The Hope of Glory

A Devotional Guide for Older Adults

Volume Two

Christ in you, the hope of glory.
COLOSSIANS 1:27

Nancy Parker Brummett

IRON
STREAM
Birmingham, Alabama

The Hope of Glory, Volume Two

Iron Stream
An imprint of Iron Stream Media
100 Missionary Ridge
Birmingham, AL 35242
IronStreamMedia.com

Iron Stream Media serves its authors as they express their views, which may not express the views of the publisher.

ISBN: 978-1-64526-370-8 (paperback)
ISBN: 978-1-64526-371-5 (e-book)

1 2 3 4 5—26 25 24 23 22
MANUFACTURED IN THE UNITED STATES OF AMERICA

Dedicated to all those
who care for older adults
with compassion and love.

Contents

Acknowledgments

As I READ THROUGH THESE lessons, so many dear older faces appear in my mind and warm my heart. They are those who attended my classes in assisted living facilities over the years and thus helped me write this book. I am grateful to them for their faithful attendance, their insights, and for being willing to tell me when a question I posed didn't make sense to them so I could rewrite it.

My gratitude extends to two women who came alongside me as this book came to fruition: Pat Beatty, who painstakingly checked and double-checked every scripture reference, and Peggy Ellis, whose expert editing pruned and polished my work. As always, I thank my husband, Jim, for his constant encouragement and support.

I am also eternally grateful to my Lord and Savior, Jesus Christ, who tapped me on the shoulder years ago to let me know my assignment was to reach out to older adults with His love and grace. It is in Him and through Him that this book was written.

Introduction and Guidelines

THE HOPE OF GLORY IS a devotional guide with fifty-seven lessons for individuals over sixty-five and those leading weekly devotional hours for older adults in retirement homes, assisted living residences, nursing homes, senior centers, or Sunday school classes. The elderly in our society too often suffer from hopelessness, loneliness, and long days separated from the people they love and the communities in which they lived and worked. *The Hope of Glory* will give them eternal hope as it communicates the gospel message and reminds them of who they are in God's eyes: not old and useless, but men and women created in His image who still have a life to live, a story to tell, and a future of eternal glory!

FOR INDIVIDUAL DEVOTIONS

If you are an older adult who would like to use *The Hope of Glory* for your daily devotions, simply work through the lessons at your own pace. Remember to turn to the back for lessons relevant to special holidays. It may help you to document your spiritual journey if you answer lesson questions in a personal journal.

FOR GROUP DEVOTIONS

To begin a class, visit a care facility near you and meet with the executive director and/or activities director. Allow them to review *The Hope of Glory* and receive their permission to go ahead. Or meet with your pastor if you are offering the class in the church. They will also help you advertise the class, determine the best time and place to meet, and gather attendees.

The Hope of Glory has been field-tested with groups of residents in assisted living facilities. Each lesson is designed to include group interaction and discussion and should take about one hour or less.

Class length may vary depending on how long it takes to assemble, the number in the group, individual participation, and the number of hymns chosen.

GUIDELINES FOR GROUP FACILITATORS

Even if you have never led a Bible study or devotional hour before, *The Hope of Glory* will make it easy for you. Your willingness and heart to serve are the most important factors. Each lesson will guide you step-by-step as you read the lesson to the group. Make sure you speak loudly enough for everyone to hear. You may use the lessons in the order they appear in the book or skip around at will. (Select the five holiday lessons in the back as needed.)

You will notice each numbered lesson has a title (reflecting the theme of the lesson), a key verse (write this on a board in the meeting room if possible), and an opening prayer. The introduction to each lesson elaborates on the theme for that class and stimulates the initial discussion period. Be willing to wait for responses to the questions. If you don't get responses to the questions as asked, try restating them in a slightly different way. As you become comfortable with the group, ask quieter individuals what they are thinking. If necessary, gently ask group members who tend to dominate the discussions to allow others a turn to share.

The scriptures and quotes are also related to the theme for each lesson. (All scripture verses are from the New International Version Study Bible, 1984, unless otherwise noted.) As you read these verses and quotes, pause after each one. If you are familiar with the verse, you might add some context from the Bible. Each entry can be a starting point for additional discussion and teaching if you would like, but this is optional and isn't necessary with each entry. Let the Holy Spirit lead the discussion. Some residents may want to bring their Bibles to the class and look up verses as you go. Of course, this is beneficial, just allow for the extra time it will take.

The meditation section of each lesson presents the biblical meaning of the theme presented and suggests behavioral or attitude change to the group as we all grow in Christ. This section will frequently present the gospel message as well, so be sensitive to group members who may want to pray privately after class to accept Jesus as their Savior. Nothing that happens is more important than this!

Each meditation will be followed by a second series of questions for discussion, a thought to share, and a suggestion for the week. Then the real fun begins as you introduce one or more suggested hymns for the group to sing together. A pianist and hymnbooks for the class would be wonderful but not necessary. Handing out copies of the words in lieu of hymnbooks increases participation. (Some attendees will want to take the words with them at the end of class.)

The hymns suggested are familiar to most, and even those who sit quietly through the discussion periods will often become animated and sing joyfully during the singing time. I will never forget the day a member of one of my classes suggested we sing "The Battle Hymn of the Republic" again—but that this time we march around the room. There we went, walkers, canes, and all! Music is important as it has the power to trigger the brain and restore memories. If you don't have accompaniment, don't hesitate to start singing and "make a joyful noise!" The class response will bless you.

After each class, ask each member in attendance for personal prayer requests or praises. This is often when you learn how each individual is really doing and what challenges he or she is facing. (Record requests to create a history of attendees and a record of what God is doing.) Close by offering these requests to the Lord—along with a lot of praise for the time you've had together. Information revealed by group members should be kept confidential unless you are concerned. Then ask their permission to share with caregivers.

Announce the theme for the next lesson to motivate group members to return. The format of *The Hope of Glory* also makes it easy for new people to join at any time.

ADDITIONAL THOUGHTS

Older adults often aren't interested in doing the homework required in traditional Bible studies. Difficulties seeing or writing may make fill-in-the-blank studies too challenging. That's why *The Hope of Glory* is designed to give them a rich, Bible-based devotional time without the hassle of books or homework.

Attendees do seem to appreciate a treat each week, however. The treat doesn't have to be anything fancy, but a plate of cookies or banana bread served with coffee or water will enhance the experience for everyone.

Another helpful addition to the class is to have something tactile to pass around in the group. For instance, for the lesson "The Solid Rock," you may want to pass around a fist-sized rock for each person to hold. For "Living in the Light," you could give each member of the class a small, battery-operated votive candle. Other takeaways are often appreciated, but remember that most residents of care facilities have limited space in their rooms.

Henri J. M. Nouwen wrote, "As long as we think that caring means only being nice and friendly to old people, paying them a visit, bringing them a flower, or offering them a ride, we are apt to forget how much more important it is for us to be willing and able to be present to those we care for. . . . Only as we enter into solidarity with the aging and speak out of common experience can we help others to discover the freedom of old age."[1]

You will find leading these sessions quite rewarding if you are comfortable with your own aging, confident in your faith, and have an attitude of humility and a sense of humor. Yet there will be days when you realize the interaction between group members was the most important reason for coming together. Be yourself and be willing to share your own experiences and spiritual journey. Soon you will develop warm relationships with those in your group, and you will be blessed as much or more than they will. Laughter and hugs go a long way to smooth over anything that may go wrong. Dispense both generously. Let the Holy Spirit be your guide, and may you sense the Lord's pleasure as you willingly serve those He loves. God bless you.

Lesson 1

Just Enough Grace

Key Verse

My grace is sufficient for you, for my power is made perfect in weakness.
2 Corinthians 12:9

Opening Prayer

O Lord, how can we ever doubt the sufficiency of Your provision for us? If we feel dry, You fill us up. If we fall down, You pick us up. You are now, and always will be, more than enough for us, Lord. Keep us ever mindful that whatever our situation, Your grace is sufficient. In the name of Jesus we pray, amen.

Introduction

Do we really appreciate the concept of having "just enough" of something? At certain times of the year in the West, residents experience a drought, so they long for the refreshing, life-giving rain to come. Once it does, they find the very sound of it soothes their souls as it dances on the rooftops, collects in the gutters, and trickles down the windowpanes.

Yet they know too much water may be worse than too little. Grim images of flooded towns in the Midwest and other parts of the country appear on TV as devastated residents strive to save themselves and anything else they can from the rising waters.

In this situation and others, we all desire "just enough," don't we? Neither too little nor too much, but just enough. In the unlikely event the rain continues in the West day after day, even residents there would no doubt complain, "When will it stop?" They want the moisture, but they want just enough to meet their needs, not so much that water becomes a problem.

Learning to identify how much is just enough is a skill many spend a lifetime developing. When we eat, can we push the plate away when we have had enough? Do we concern ourselves about whether we have enough money, or clothing, or time? Believing that God, through His grace, will provide just enough of everything we need can bring great peace to our hearts and minds. When we trust Him for our provision, we never have to worry about having enough again.

For Reflection or Discussion

- Were you ever in the position of having too little of something you needed? What were your needs and how were they met?
- Were you ever in the position of having too much of something you thought you needed? What was it, and what was the result?
- Have you learned to be satisfied with "just enough" in your life? If so, please explain.

Scriptures and Quotes

Yet the Lord longs to be gracious to you; he rises to show you compassion.
Isaiah 30:18

When he arrived and saw the evidence of the grace of God, he was glad and encouraged them all to remain true to the Lord with all their hearts.
Acts 11:23

And God is able to make all grace abound to you, so that in all things at all times, having all that you need, you will abound in every good work.
2 Corinthians 9:8

But to each one of us grace has been given as Christ apportioned it.
Ephesians 4:7

But if we have food and clothing, we will be content with that.
I TIMOTHY 6:8

Command those who are rich in this present world not to be arrogant nor to put their hope in wealth, which is so uncertain, but to put their hope in God, who richly provides us with everything for our enjoyment.
I TIMOTHY 6:17

Grace and peace be yours in abundance through the knowledge of God and of Jesus our Lord.
2 PETER 1:2

Grace is but glory begun, and glory is but grace perfected.
JONATHAN EDWARDS

Never lose sight of the fact that old age needs so little but needs that little so much.[2]
MARGARET WILLOUR

MEDITATION

In truth, we must be patient and wait for just enough of God's grace to fall upon us. So we pray, Lord, give me just enough patience to deal with this situation, but don't let it drag on forever. Give me just enough wealth to meet my needs—not so much that money becomes a burden, nor so little that money becomes a challenge, but just enough. Just enough hope to get through each day, just enough well-being, just enough wisdom, the list goes on.

Yet the only thing we can be absolutely sure we will always have just enough of is God's grace. When the Apostle Paul pleaded with God to take away the thorn in his flesh, God replied, *"My grace is sufficient for you, for my power is made perfect in weakness"* (2 Corinthians 12:9).

God in His goodness sheds His common grace generously over all His creation, but to those who trust in Him, he adds the promise they will always have just enough grace. Sometimes, in the midst of disaster or a heartbreaking situation, His grace can feel like a mere trickle. But looking back, we realize it was indeed just the grace we needed, just when we needed it. Other times it feels as if God is pouring out an abundance of His grace on us—letting grace overflow into every parched portion of our souls. Always, in any circumstance, His grace is just enough. Let's not miss God's grace, whether it comes as a sprinkle or a deluge.

FOR REFLECTION OR DISCUSSION

- In what way can having too much of something be a burden?
- Why do you think God is so consistent in giving us just enough of what we need, just when we need it?
- Is there a time you can look back on and see, retrospectively, that God provided just the grace you needed?

A THOUGHT TO SHARE

Grace is a gift from God. It is His unmerited favor.

SUGGESTION FOR THE WEEK

Spend some time evaluating your present circumstances. Where can you see that God provided just enough?

SUGGESTED HYMNS

- Amazing Grace
- Grace Greater Than Our Sin

PRAYER REQUESTS AND CLOSING PRAYER

LESSON 2

Take Time to Be Holy

KEY VERSE

But just as he who called you is holy, so be holy in all you do; for it is written: "Be holy, because I am holy."
I PETER 1:15–16

OPENING PRAYER

O GOD, WE COME BEFORE YOU today woefully aware of our innate lack of holiness. Only You are holy, Lord: You and You alone. How grateful we are that You impart Your holiness to us. Because of the sacrifice of Your Son for us, we are also able to live holy lives, and so we thank You. In Jesus' name we pray, amen.

INTRODUCTION

Of all the ways we choose to describe ourselves to others, "holy" is probably not an adjective that quickly comes to mind. When we meet someone for the first time, we may tell them our name, where we live, where we grew up, even what we do or did for a living, but it's not likely we would describe ourselves as holy. If we did introduce ourselves that way, the other person would no doubt turn and walk the other way, totally put off by our lack of humility.

Our reluctance to describe ourselves as holy stems from our knowledge of every selfish, unkind, unholy thing we have ever done in life. Perhaps someone who has given his or her entire life to the church or to working in the mission field might be holy, we surmise, but not us. Not someone who has lived an ordinary life of work, rearing a family, and going about daily chores—and making his or her share of mistakes.

We are also hesitant to describe ourselves as holy because we don't want people to believe we think we are superior to them in some way. We don't want to cast a holier-than-thou shadow across our relationship with them. Yet the Bible assures us that once we believe in God and accept Jesus Christ as our Savior, the perfect holiness that is God's alone can be ours as well. We merely need to focus on God's holiness and take time to be holy in His presence.

FOR REFLECTION OR DISCUSSION

- What does being holy mean to you?
- Is there someone you know who you would describe as holy? Why do they come to mind?
- Do you think of yourself as holy? Why or why not?

SCRIPTURES AND QUOTES

*Worship the LORD in the splendor of his holiness;
tremble before him, all the earth.*
PSALM 96:9

But now that you have been set free from sin and have become slaves to God, the benefit you reap leads to holiness, and the result is eternal life.
ROMANS 6:22

For he chose us in him before the creation of the world to be holy and blameless in his sight.
EPHESIANS 1:4

But join me in suffering for the gospel, by the power of God, who has saved us and called us to a holy life—not because of anything we have done but because of his own purpose and grace.
2 TIMOTHY 1:8–9

*By one sacrifice he has made perfect forever those
who are being made holy.*
HEBREWS 10:14

*Make every effort to live in peace with all men and to be holy; without
holiness no one will see the Lord.*
HEBREWS 12:14

*A commitment to holiness means having a life that is always "ready for
company" and open for inspection—a life that can stand up to scrutiny—
not just in the obvious things, but in the hidden places where most might
not think to look.³*
NANCY LEIGH DeMOSS

*A holy life is not an ascetic, or gloomy, or solitary life, but a life regulated
by divine truth and faithful in Christian duty.—It is living above the
world while we are still in it.*
TRYON EDWARDS

*It is a great deal better to live a holy life than to talk about it.
Lighthouses do not ring bells and fire cannon to call attention to their
shining—they just shine.⁴*
DWIGHT L. MOODY

MEDITATION

Waking up each morning with the goal to be holy in all we say
and do could be a bit daunting. Yet when we realize that, as believers,
we already have God's holiness through His Spirit within us, then we
only need to say no to anything that doesn't reflect God's holiness and
yes to anything that does.

We can begin by looking at how we prioritize our time. Do we
waste time on TV shows and then say we have no time for God? Or
do we make time to be holy by spending quiet time in prayer with
the Lord, reading His Word, and going to Him in prayer? He will be
honored, and we will be blessed, if we spend time with Him.

How about the way we respond to the world around us? Are our
words kind, lifting others up, or are they hurtful? Are we more likely
to grumble over the inconveniences of life or to praise God despite

them? The choice is ours to make each and every day. When we make the holy choices, we are not only living a holier life here on earth, but we are preparing ourselves for the completely holy life we will have in heaven someday.

The older we get, the less impact we may feel we have on the world, but we can all reflect God's holiness into the lives of others. When we demonstrate grace under pressure, mercy, forgiveness, faith, or hope, we expose our families and communities to God's holiness.

"I heard a story about an elderly woman who would sit in silence for hours in her rocking chair, hands folded in her lap, eyes gazing off into the far distance. One day her daughter asked, 'Mother, what do you think about when you sit there so quietly?' Her mother replied softly with a twinkle in her eye, 'That's just between Jesus and me.'"[5] This woman took the time to be holy and so can we. Each day we can choose to reflect God's holiness to a hurting world. He promises us His holiness is in us. We just have to let this holiness out.

FOR REFLECTION OR DISCUSSION

- What could you do today to reflect God's holiness and let it shine into the life of another?
- To be holy is to be set apart. Is there at least a portion of each day that you set apart to spend time with God? When and how do you take time to be holy?
- Unconfessed, unforgiven sins keep us from feeling holy. When you examine your heart, do any such sins come to mind? Confess them today.

A THOUGHT TO SHARE

We all make time for what matters most to us. Take time to be holy.

Suggestion for the Week

Look for the holy in the ordinary events of this week. Where is God being honored? Join in these activities. Take time to bask in His holiness and thank Him for imparting His holiness to you.

Suggested Hymns

- Holy, Holy, Holy
- Take Time to Be Holy

Prayer Requests and Closing Prayer

LESSON 3

Finding Fellowship

KEY VERSE

For where two or three come together in my name, there am I with them.
MATTHEW 18:20

OPENING PRAYER

O LORD, HOW WE LONG TO be in fellowship with You. To sit at Your feet and listen to Your teaching. To walk with You and talk with You. To know You are with us in every situation in our lives. Thank You for making such fellowship possible as we come to You and as we find You in others we encounter. In Your holy name we pray, amen.

INTRODUCTION

We think of fellowship as the condition of sharing similar interests, ideals, or experiences, as by reason of profession, religion, or nationality, or as the companionship of peers in a congenial atmosphere. We all desire fellowship of one kind or another, whether we realize it or not. People were designed to connect with other people. All of us are wiser, happier, and more fulfilled when we experience life in the company of others. No wonder then that we seek a connection through the shared experience of fellowship.

Certainly, those who live in care centers have plenty of opportunity to connect with others, yet when the people who surround you are there by chance, not necessarily by choice, making meaningful connections can be difficult. The spirit of openness and intimacy that creates true fellowship can be hard to come by at times, if at all.

Yet there's no reason to become discouraged. Even fellowship with one other person who shares your beliefs and values can make each day more meaningful and joyful. Finding a whole group of like-minded, like-hearted folks is truly a blessing.

Sometimes the more we reach out to others, the more fellowship we create. But we can still have fellowship with the Lord even when we don't find other people with whom we can commune. How amazing it is that He is never too busy to communicate with us or to listen to what's on our hearts. Fellowship with the Almighty is blessed fellowship indeed.

For Reflection or Discussion

- Do you have people with whom you enjoy spending time each day?
- Why do you think some people shy away from joining in fellowship with others?
- Do you often seek out others with whom to fellowship? Why or why not?

Scriptures and Quotes

How good and pleasant it is when brothers live together in unity!
Psalm 133:1

*God, who has called you into fellowship with his
Son Jesus Christ our Lord, is faithful.*
1 Corinthians 1:9

*May the grace of the Lord Jesus Christ, and the love of God, and the
fellowship of the Holy Spirit be with you all.*
2 Corinthians 13:14

*I want to know Christ and the power of his resurrection and the
fellowship of sharing in his sufferings, becoming like him in his death,
and so, somehow, to attain to the resurrection from the dead.*
Philippians 3:10–11

*Let us not give up meeting together, as some are in
the habit of doing, but let us encourage one another—
and all the more as you see the Day approaching.*
HEBREWS 10:25

*We proclaim to you what we have seen and heard, so that
you also may have fellowship with us. And our fellowship
is with the Father and with his Son, Jesus Christ.*
1 JOHN 1:3

*If we claim to have fellowship with him yet walk in the darkness, we lie
and do not live by the truth. But if we walk in the light, as he is in the
light, we have fellowship with one another, and the blood of Jesus, his
Son, purifies us from all sin.*
1 JOHN 1:6–7

*We are not sanctified for ourselves, we are called into the fellowship of
the Gospel, and things happen which have nothing to do with us, God is
getting us into fellowship with Himself.*[6]
OSWALD CHAMBERS

MEDITATION

Throughout the Christian church, many congregations stand on
Sunday mornings and recite an old creed of the church, The Apostles'
Creed. A portion of that creed reads: "I believe in the Holy Ghost,
the holy catholic church, the communion of saints, the forgiveness of
sins, the resurrection of the body, and the life everlasting." (The word
catholic here refers not to the Roman Catholic Church but to the
universal church of the Lord Jesus Christ.)

What do we mean when we say we believe in the communion
of saints? While the term can have deep and debatable theological
meaning, certainly in part the "communion of saints" is the fellowship
that believers enjoy with one another here on earth.

What binds us together so strongly? Clearly it is the Lord Jesus
Himself and the belief we share that He is present with us. When we
seek fellowship, or communion, with others, we are seeking Christ,
aren't we? We see Christ in the light of their eyes or the kindness of

their touch, and that awareness draws us into fellowship with them as nothing else ever can.

Be aware of those in your circle of influence who share your belief in Jesus Christ and, like you, long to fellowship with others who know Him. Don't be afraid to share what you believe with others, for to do so is to give them the gift of eternal life if they accept God's grace for themselves. How sweet it is to fellowship with one another and to feel the presence of the Lord when we do.

For Reflection or Discussion

- Have you ever been immediately drawn to someone you met only to learn later they share your love for the Lord?
- Why do you think it's so easy for us to fellowship with other believers, even if they seem very different from us in appearance or life experience?
- What can you do to grow the community of fellowship where you live?

A Thought to Share

The tie that binds is not only blessed, it's eternal.

Suggestion for the Week

Ask the Lord to reveal to you those in your midst who share your faith in Him. Then together you can begin to build a life-giving fellowship of believers.

Suggested Hymns

- Blest Be the Tie That Binds
- Leaning on the Everlasting Arms
- The Church's One Foundation

Prayer Requests and Closing Prayer

LESSON 4

But God

KEY VERSE

*My flesh and my heart may fail, but God is the strength
of my heart and my portion forever.*
PSALM 73:26

OPENING PRAYER

ALMIGHTY GOD, HOW WE WELCOME Your involvement in our
lives. Just when things look the bleakest, You so often step in to
change the situation entirely. When we look back over our lives, we
see so clearly the times when You intervened for our good. Take away
our doubt, O God. May we rest in the knowledge that You are in
control and will intervene in our lives whenever You choose. In the
name of Jesus we pray, amen.

INTRODUCTION

When things aren't going well, we often look around for a
superhero to save the day, don't we? Hollywood and television
producers have made a lot of money with movies and programs
featuring daring, multi-skilled miracle men and women: Batman,
Spiderman, Wonder Woman; the list goes on and on. A favorite
childhood cartoon character of many baby boomers was Mighty
Mouse! We were eager to believe that even this small, insignificant
mouse could possess the superpowers needed to save the day.

What about now? Do you ever feel the need for someone, or something, to swoop into your life and rescue you from the stresses and challenges of everyday life? As our own personal capabilities diminish, it's common for us to look for someone else to provide the strength, or the wisdom, or the emotional fortitude we lack.

How comforting then to read through the Bible and see all the times God intervened in people's lives to improve their situations and to save them. We may all have difficult stories to share of certain times of our lives, but believers in God so often find that the words *but God* introduce what happened to make things better. "I was so lonely," one might say, "*but God* brought a new friend into my life." "I didn't know where my next meal was coming from," we may hear, "*but God* provided for all my needs." What a privilege it is to know an active, living God who is more powerful than any superhero. He can and will intervene in our lives just when we need Him the most.

FOR REFLECTION OR DISCUSSION

- Who have been the heroes in your life?
- When was the last time you hoped someone would swoop into a situation and make a difference?
- Is there a time you can remember when you are sure God intervened to save you or reverse your circumstances?

SCRIPTURES AND QUOTES

You intended to harm me, but God intended it for good to accomplish what is now being done, the saving of many lives.
GENESIS 50:20

But God will redeem my life from the grave; he will surely take me to himself.
PSALM 49:15

But God demonstrates his own love for us in this: While we were still sinners, Christ died for us.
ROMANS 5:8

However, as it is written: "No eye has seen, no ear has heard, no mind has conceived what God has prepared for those who love him"—but God has revealed it to us by his Spirit.

1 CORINTHIANS 2:9–10

In all his dispensations God is at work for our good.

ANONYMOUS

There is something in the nature of things which the mind of man, which reason, which human power cannot effect. . . . What can this be but God?

CICERO

Cast all your cares on God; that anchor holds.

ALFRED, LORD TENNYSON

MEDITATION

Of course, God's greatest intervention for all people for all time was when He sent His Son to die for our sins. Sin entered the world, making it impossible for the people God created to be united with Him in heaven. *But God* had a plan. He sent Jesus Christ to die for our sins so we could stand faultless before Him someday. His death was the most beautiful and powerful intervention imaginable.

Yet as we wait for the day when we will be united with God for all eternity, we can long for His presence here on earth, too, can't we? Beth Lueders wrote a book about waiting on God titled *Two Days Longer*, a reference to how long it took Jesus to come to the aid of Mary and Martha after their brother Lazarus became ill and died. In the book, Beth interviews an elderly woman who asks, "Dear, do you know the most powerful words in all the Bible?" When Beth says she isn't sure, the woman responds, "But God! You know why? Because when situations look their worst and we are weary from waiting, God steps in and proves that he is all-powerful, loving, and wise."[7]

We all want to get to the "but God" point sooner rather than later, don't we? Yet a good thing to do while we wait is to review all the "but God" experiences in our lives and the lives of others. Moses thought he and the Israelites were goners for sure, *but God* parted the Red Sea. Joseph was sold into slavery in a foreign land, *but God* elevated him to a position that allowed him to save many lives, including those of his father and brothers.

Never underestimate what God can do. He is the ultimate superhero, the quintessential Savior. When you tell others the story of your life, remember to include all the times God intervened. In the process, share the good news that we were all dead in our sin, *but God* gave us eternal life through His Son Jesus Christ.

FOR REFLECTION OR DISCUSSION

- It's tempting for us to take credit for what God has done, isn't it? Do you need to revise a story you tell about your life to include the phrase "but God"?
- How do you call on God when you know you need His intervention in a difficult situation?
- How long are you willing to wait for God to intervene?

A THOUGHT TO SHARE

We are weak, but God is all powerful!

SUGGESTION FOR THE WEEK

The ability to see God's intervention at work can be a gift to others. This week if someone shares a problem or concern, remind him or her not to leave God out of the equation.

SUGGESTED HYMNS

- God of Grace and God of Glory
- I Sing the Mighty Power of God
- Rock of Ages

PRAYER REQUESTS AND CLOSING PRAYER

LESSON 5

It's a Mystery!

KEY VERSE

To them God has chosen to make known among the Gentiles the glorious riches of this mystery, which is Christ in you, the hope of glory.
COLOSSIANS 1:27

OPENING PRAYER

ALMIGHTY GOD, THERE IS SO much we don't understand. We study Your Word and we pray, but we know so much of life will be a mystery to us until we see You face to face. And yet, we trust You as the Author and Creator of all. Thank You for the mysteries you have revealed to us and for the revelations yet to come. In the name of Jesus we pray, amen.

INTRODUCTION

Often children ask insightful questions about the world around them that adults find difficult to answer. In the absence of a sound explanation about the heavens or the deep sea, adults often resort to the age-old answer, "It's a mystery." That usually satisfies the child until the adult can formulate a better answer.

We all love a good mystery, don't we? Most anyone over fifty remembers curling up on a summer afternoon with a Nancy Drew or Hardy Boys mystery as a child. As we got older, it might have been Agatha Christie or Robert Ludlum who kept us captivated. A good mystery is engaging because of the challenge posed for us to figure out "who done it," as they say. Good mystery plots translate well to stage plays and movie scripts as well. Yes, everyone loves a good mystery.

Yet some of the mysteries we encounter in life aren't quite so entertaining. The twists and turns they take, the plot developments if you will, don't always lead us to a logical, acceptable ending like a good mystery novel does. Rather, we may live out our days never really understanding why a relationship failed, why someone we love must die unexpectedly, or why we are still around wondering why.

Blessedly, we don't have to wonder any longer than it takes for us to turn the questions over to Jesus, *the author and perfecter of our faith* (Hebrews 12:2). Sometimes He will choose to reveal the answer to the mystery to us. Other times He will ask us to wait just a bit longer, when all will be revealed, all mysteries solved.

For Reflection or Discussion

- Did you enjoy reading mysteries as a child? Do you read them still? Which authors are your favorites?
- If you read mysteries, what do you enjoy most about a good mystery? What do you like least?
- Do you have mysteries in your own life? How or when do you think they will be resolved?

Scriptures and Quotes

*During the night the mystery was revealed to Daniel in a vision.
Then Daniel praised the God of heaven and said . . .
"He reveals deep and hidden things; he knows what
lies in darkness, and light dwells with him."*
Daniel 2:19, 22

*I praise you, Father, Lord of heaven and earth, because you
have hidden these things from the wise and learned,
and revealed them to little children.*
Matthew 11:25

*Now to him who is able to establish you by my gospel and the
proclamation of Jesus Christ, according to the revelation of the mystery*

hidden for long ages past, but now revealed and made known through the prophetic writings by the command of the eternal God, so that all nations might believe and obey him—to the only wise God be glory forever through Jesus Christ! Amen.
ROMANS 16:25–27

Listen, I tell you a mystery: We will not all sleep, but we will all be changed—in a flash, in the twinkling of an eye, at the last trumpet. For the trumpet will sound, the dead will be raised imperishable, and we will be changed.
1 CORINTHIANS 15:51–52

This mystery is that through the gospel the Gentiles are heirs together with Israel, members together of one body, and sharers together in the promise in Christ Jesus.
EPHESIANS 3:6

"For this reason a man will leave his father and mother and be united to his wife, and the two will become one flesh." This is a profound mystery— but I am talking about Christ and the church.
EPHESIANS 5:31–32

Pray also for me, that whenever I open my mouth, words may be given me so that I will fearlessly make known the mystery of the gospel, for which I am an ambassador in chains. Pray that I may declare it fearlessly, as I should.
EPHESIANS 6:19–20

My purpose is that they may be encouraged in heart and united in love, so that they may have the full riches of complete understanding, in order that they may know the mystery of God, namely, Christ, in whom are hidden all the treasures of wisdom and knowledge.
COLOSSIANS 2:2–3

Beyond all question, the mystery of godliness is great: He appeared in a body, was vindicated by the Spirit, was seen by angels, was preached among the nations, was believed on in the world, was taken up in glory.
1 TIMOTHY 3:16

In due time He will reveal the treasures of the unknown to you—the riches of the glory of the mystery. Recognize that the mystery is simply the veil covering God's face.[8]

L. B. COWMAN

MEDITATION

The best-selling book of all time, the Holy Bible, will never be catalogued as a mystery book, and yet it is full of mysterious stories and plots, isn't it? From Genesis to Revelation, we read accounts that leave us asking, "But how could that be?" And yet because we believe that the Bible is God's Word, we know that even the most mysterious parts will be perfectly clear to us one day.

What one calls a miracle, someone else might call a mystery. The parting of the Red Sea, the casting of demons into pigs, the raising of Lazarus from the dead—these accounts and others rely more on our faith than our logic, don't they? And yet we aren't always left wondering about the rest of the story.

The Apostle Paul writes often about the revelation of the greatest mystery of all. We aren't left wondering who Jesus was and what He came to do for us because God in His goodness decided to completely reveal this to us through His holy Word. Not only does He reveal that Jesus is fully man and fully divine, but He lets us know that Jesus came to die for our sins so we might have eternal life (John 3:16). Beyond that amazing truth God reveals the grander mystery, the bigger picture of how all things in heaven and earth will be unified under Christ someday (Ephesians 1:10).

Whenever we find ourselves wrestling with solving a mystery in our lives, we need to remember how God chose to reveal His most wonderful mysteries to us. In His time He will provide the solution to every mystery we wrestle with. Then, when we see Him face to face, all things will be revealed for our complete satisfaction and His glory.

FOR REFLECTION OR DISCUSSION

- What Biblical mysteries confound you the most? In other words, what are the first things you want to ask God about when you see Him?

- Is there a mystery in your life you are currently working on solving?
- How does it feel to know God will solve it someday? Does that knowledge give you peace?

A Thought to Share

> *The Old Testament is the new concealed;*
> *the New Testament is the old revealed.*

Suggestion for the Week

Spend some time reflecting on life's mysteries. Whatever you can't solve, especially a mystery in your own life, take it to God. He will give you the solution in His time.

Suggested Hymns

- Have Thine Own Way, Lord
- To God Be the Glory

Prayer Requests and Closing Prayer

Lesson 6

Being Like Jesus

Key Verse

And we, who with unveiled faces all reflect the Lord's glory,
are being transformed into his likeness with ever-increasing glory,
which comes from the Lord, who is the Spirit.
2 Corinthians 3:18

Opening Prayer

O Lord Jesus, we know we can never be completely like You, and yet, through the power of the Holy Spirit, we can reflect Your light and love into the world. Fill us up, Lord, and help us to live more like You every day. In Your name we pray, amen.

Introduction

How often we try to imitate someone we admire. Young girls want to dress and sing like their favorite pop stars, sometimes to the consternation of their parents. Young football and baseball players watch closely the behaviors of their favorite sports heroes, on and off the field, and try to be like them. Years ago, a commercial recognized this tendency and created the advertising slogan "Be like Mike" in reference to Michael Jordan. It was only a slogan, but millions evidently hoped wearing T-shirts and shoes with the Michael Jordan brand would miraculously make it possible for them to dunk a basketball like Mike.

Perhaps all of us with older siblings can remember how painfully we wanted to be like our older brother or sister. One woman remembers sneaking into her older sister's room when she was away. She didn't want to take anything; she just wanted to smear on a bit of her sister's lipstick, smell her sister's perfume, and maybe try on a blouse or skirt her sister wore.

And what little child doesn't imitate his or her parent at some point in time? Little boys even adopt the stride of their dads, attempting to be just like them, and often cheer for the same teams their dads love. Little girls love to clomp around in their mothers' high heels or play in their makeup. It's natural for us to imitate someone we admire.

But we need to be careful who we decide to imitate, don't we? Parents know that the role models their children choose can have a huge influence over how they behave. How blessed we are as believers in Jesus Christ that we have the perfect role model to imitate. Maybe we can't "Be like Mike," but through the power of the Holy Spirit, all who believe can be more like Jesus.

FOR REFLECTION OR DISCUSSION

- Who did you admire the most when you were growing up?
- In what ways did you try to be like him or her?
- Has anyone in your life ever tried to be like you?

SCRIPTURES AND QUOTES

So God created man in his own image, in the image of God he created him; male and female he created them.
GENESIS 1:27

For those God foreknew he also predestined to be conformed to the likeness of his Son.
ROMANS 8:29

Those who belong to Christ Jesus have crucified the sinful nature with its passions and desires.
GALATIANS 5:24

Your attitude should be the same as that of Christ Jesus: Who, being in very nature God, did not consider equality with God something to be grasped, but made himself nothing, taking the very nature of a servant, being made in human likeness. And being found in appearance as a man, he humbled himself and became obedient to death—even death on a cross!
PHILIPPIANS 2:5–8

You became imitators of us and of the Lord; in spite of severe suffering, you welcomed the message with the joy given by the Holy Spirit.
1 THESSALONIANS 1:6

But we know that when he appears, we shall be like him, for we shall see him as he is.
1 JOHN 3:2

More about Jesus I would know,
More of His grace to others show;
More of His saving fullness see,
More of His love who died for me.
E. E. HEWITT

Jesus Christ, the condescension of divinity, and the exaltation of humanity.
PHILLIPS BROOKS

The one marvelous secret of a holy life lies not in imitating Jesus, but in letting the perfections of Jesus manifest themselves in my mortal flesh. Sanctification is "Christ in you." [9]
OSWALD CHAMBERS

MEDITATION

The Bible promises us that we were created in the image of God. Only human beings have this distinction. No one knows what God's physical appearance is, but through reading the Word we know His characteristics. Because we are created in His image, we too can demonstrate love, wisdom, and justice.

Believers in God's Son, Jesus Christ, have the best opportunity to reflect the Divine. Once we believe in Jesus, the Holy Spirit indwells us. It is then through the power of the Holy Spirit that we can be imitators of Christ. We become His hands and feet in the world as we reach out to help or comfort those who need more of Jesus in their lives.

Since we have this incredible power, how else can we be more like Jesus? The answer is found in the Bible. In Galatians 2:20, Paul writes, *"I have been crucified with Christ and I no longer live, but Christ lives in me. The life I live in the body, I live by faith in the Son of God, who loved me and gave himself for me."* To be crucified with Christ is to set aside all selfish desires and motives and simply allow Jesus to live out His life through us. We must do this to be more like Him, and He will help us. Jesus modeled how we are to work and live together. Now He continues to guide us through the Holy Bible, through prayer, and through the Counselor, the Holy Spirit, whom He sent to help us.

Christian scholars suggest there are several things which contribute to our becoming more like Christ. First, we must examine our lives to see if there is any unconfessed sin blocking our ability to reflect Christ's love and forgiveness. If so, we must confess and repent. Also, we must be willing to surrender all to the Lord and to declare along with John the Baptist, *"He must become greater; I must become less"* (John 3:30). As we continue to guard our hearts and minds in Christ Jesus and grow in our understanding of who He was and what He came to do for us, then we will be more like Him each day we live. Others will be able to see Jesus as we allow His light to shine through us.

For Reflection or Discussion

- Have you ever said or done something that you know for a fact could not have occurred without the intervening power of the Holy Spirit?
- Is there anything in your life now that may be blocking your ability to be like Christ as you move through your day?
- How can we be more Christlike to others in the midst of our present circumstances?

A Thought to Share

We will never be completely like Christ, but we can be Christlike.

SUGGESTION FOR THE WEEK

Pray and ask the Lord to show you an opportunity to be His hands and feet to another person this week. Do whatever He reveals. You may be the only chance someone else will have to see Him.

SUGGESTED HYMNS

- Give Me Jesus
- I Want to Be Like Jesus
- Lord, I Want to Be a Christian

PRAYER REQUESTS AND CLOSING PRAYER

LESSON 7

God Is Good

KEY VERSE

> *I am still confident of this: I will see the goodness of the LORD*
> *in the land of the living. Wait for the LORD; be strong*
> *and take heart and wait for the LORD.*
> PSALM 27:13–14

OPENING PRAYER

ALMIGHTY GOD, WE NEVER WANT to doubt Your goodness to us, but sometimes it can feel like You are looking the other way or not noticing what's happening. Reassure us, Father God. Remind us that even when we don't see Your hand at work, You are always working for our good. In Jesus' name we pray, amen.

INTRODUCTION

What is good to one person may not be good to another. Your favorite meal may be fried liver and onions, while your friend would eat anything but. You may wait with great anticipation for the first leaves to fall, signaling the approach of autumn, while someone else you know prefers to hold on to summer for as long as possible. You may have a TV program you try not to miss that your roommate finds annoying. We can't always agree on what is good because we are different, with different tastes and preferences.

We can't even always agree on what constitutes good behavior. The culture we live in accepts some behaviors as good that we grew up believing were bad. For instance, more couples are living together without getting married than ever before, and many of them have babies. Often, we clash with members of younger generations, even those in our own families, because we have different beliefs and understandings about what good behavior should look like.

We always fall short no matter how hard we try to be good. Like the Apostle Paul, we do those things we shouldn't and leave undone that which we should do (Romans 7:19). We forget an important appointment or that we agreed to meet a friend at a certain time. We slip into old habits of gossiping or being critical of others, and later we say to ourselves, "Well, that wasn't good of me."

The truth is there is only One who is good all the time, and that is God. We may not always understand Him, but we can always trust Him. God is good all the time.

FOR REFLECTION OR DISCUSSION

- What foods do you think of as good that others might not enjoy?
- Were there people who influenced your thoughts about good versus bad behavior? Who were they?
- Why do you think it's difficult for any of us to be good all the time?

SCRIPTURES AND QUOTES

Give thanks to the LORD, for he is good; his love endures forever.
I CHRONICLES 16:34

Taste and see that the LORD is good; blessed is the man who takes refuge in him.
PSALM 34:8

The LORD is good, a refuge in times of trouble. He cares for those who trust in him.
NAHUM 1:7

You are good and what you do is good; teach me your decrees.
PSALM 119:68

The LORD *is good to all; he has compassion on all he has made.*
PSALM 145:9

A certain ruler asked him, "Good teacher, what must I do to inherit eternal life?" "Why do you call me good?" Jesus answered. "No one is good—except God alone."
LUKE 18:18–19

And we know that in all things God works for the good of those who love him, who have been called according to his purpose.
ROMANS 8:28

God is great, and therefore He will be sought: He is good, and therefore He will be found.
ANONYMOUS

I believe in God and in his Wisdom and Benevolence.
JOHN ADAMS

God is great, God is good, and we thank him for our food.
CHILDREN'S PRAYER

MEDITATION

In *The Lion, the Witch and the Wardrobe*, one of The Chronicles of Narnia books by C. S. Lewis, the character Aslan is a strong and mighty lion who represents Jesus Christ in the story. When the children ask Mr. and Mrs. Beaver about Aslan, and they find out he's a lion, they become concerned. "Then he isn't safe?" Lucy asks. "'Course he isn't safe," Mr. Beaver says. "But he's good. He's the King, I tell you."[10]

In so many ways this describes our good God, doesn't it? We know He is powerful beyond words and capable of causing the very end of the world as we know it should He choose to do so. And yet we trust Him because we know that in addition to being almighty and all powerful, He is also full of compassion, He is just, and yes, He is very good.

We can never measure up to God's goodness. Even when we do something good, we often brag about what we did, proving we aren't purely good at all. The best way to recognize our need for a Savior may be to compare our goodness to God's. God knew from the beginning that we could never measure up. That's why He sent Jesus to die for our sins and close the gap between us and God.

At times, when tragedy and confusion cause you to question God's goodness, reflect back over everything you know of His character. We can't always see what God is doing or why, but we must never question His goodness to us. You can trust God because God is good.

For Reflection or Discussion

- Was there a time in your life when you didn't understand what God was doing or where He was?
- Have you ever questioned God's goodness?
- Share a time when you did something good but gave God the glory.

A Thought to Share

God may not always be understood, but He's always good.

Suggestion for the Week

In your conversations with others, remind them of God's goodness to them. Ask them to think back over all the blessings in their lives.

Suggested Hymns

- How Great Thou Art
- God Is So Good
- Good Good Father

Prayer Requests and Closing Prayer

LESSON 8

Lord, I'm Lonely

KEY VERSE

*Hear my voice when I call, O LORD; be merciful to me and answer me.
My heart says of you, "Seek his face!" Your face, LORD, I will seek.*
PSALM 27:7–8

OPENING PRAYER

O LORD, IT CAN BE HARD for us to confess to You that there are
days when we feel lonely. We know You have provided for our needs
and surrounded us with people, yet still there's a sense of loneliness
that can come over us, Lord. Be especially close to us in those times.
Assure us that You are never far from us. In Your name we pray, amen.

INTRODUCTION

It's hard for us to give ourselves permission to feel lonely, isn't it?
Yet even if we are blessed to be a part of a large family or to live in a
community with a lot of other people, we can still experience loneliness.

All of us have times in our lives when we spend time alone, and
many of us are created to really need time to ourselves. Young adults
may move to a distant city to take a job and end up living alone in
a small apartment. Although it feels strange at first, they may decide
that living alone has its benefits. A young mother sends her last
child off to school and finds she can have some time alone—and she
welcomes it. And older adults, through any number of circumstances,
may find they are once again living alone.

Psychologists and counselors tell us there's a big difference between being alone and feeling lonely, however. Being alone is not so bad if we've learned to appreciate our own company. However, when we are lonely, no amount of activity or diversion can fill the deep aching we feel right down to our bones. We can feel lonely in a crowd, or even in a relationship, if we don't allow ourselves to open up to intimacy with others.

We often keep our lonely feelings to ourselves because we believe admitting we are lonely can seem self-focused and ungrateful. Soon one lonely day turns into two, and the days to weeks and months.

Life doesn't have to be that way! Feeling lonely from time to time is natural. Once we have Jesus in our lives, we may choose to be alone, but we never have to be lonely.

FOR REFLECTION OR DISCUSSION

- Are you the type of person who enjoys having some alone time? If so, how do you spend it?
- Does your alone time ever lead to loneliness?
- If so, what do you do to combat the feeling of loneliness?

SCRIPTURES AND QUOTES

God sets the lonely in families.
PSALM 68:6

But Jesus often withdrew to lonely places and prayed.
LUKE 5:16

I no longer call you servants, because a servant does not know his master's business. Instead, I have called you friends, for everything that I learned from my Father I have made known to you.
JOHN 15:15

"You believe at last!" Jesus answered. "But a time is coming, and has come, when you will be scattered, each to his own home. You will leave me all alone. Yet I am not alone, for my Father is with me."
JOHN 16:31–32

Father, I want those you have given me to be with me where I am, and to see my glory, the glory you have given me because you loved me before the creation of the world.

JOHN 17:24

Alone with God! It is there that what is hid with God is made known—God's ideals, God's hopes, God's doings.[11]

OSWALD CHAMBERS

Loneliness and the feeling of being unwanted is the most terrible poverty.[12]

MOTHER TERESA

MEDITATION

Do you think Jesus was ever lonely during His ministry on earth? The Bible mentions many times when He withdrew to a place of solitude to be alone and pray, but do you think He ever felt lonely? Surely, He felt removed from the heavenly realms as He assumed His life as a man, and He was utterly alone when He went to the cross to die for our sins. But during His life on earth, He was first part of a family, then surrounded by a group of disciples with whom He could share His most intimate thoughts and fears. In His human form, He showed us both how to be purposefully alone for a time and how to surround ourselves with others for the purpose of community and fellowship.

Time spent alone by choice can rejuvenate us, especially if we are introverted by nature. When we spend our alone time in prayer or gathering our energy and thoughts, then we can be ready to connect with others at a higher level of engagement and purpose. Yet too many alone days in a row can result in loneliness, can't they? And studies show that too much loneliness can result in depression, which can not only make us miserable but shorten our lives as well.

How do we combat loneliness? As people of faith, we can do what Jesus did and surround ourselves with a community of people who care for us. We can let down the emotional walls that keep us isolated. We are less lonely the more we share on an intimate level with someone else, speaking and listening with our hearts. Jesus wants to be that friend who is always available. He wants to be the one we always allow behind the emotional walls we build. He wants to enjoy our company and to delight in our enjoyment of Him.

Take time to be alone when you need to, but don't let loneliness lead you down a path of depression and isolation. Open your heart to Jesus first, then to others in your family or community. You'll be so glad you did.

FOR REFLECTION OR DISCUSSION

- Share a time when you felt lonely. Did something happen to change your situation?
- How can we accept responsibility for our own loneliness?
- If you believe in Jesus, He calls you His friend. How does His intimate friendship with you keep you from feeling lonely?

A THOUGHT TO SHARE

Opening your heart to others is the best cure for loneliness.

SUGGESTION FOR THE WEEK

Take note of the time you spend alone. Is it too much or just enough? If you feel lonely, reach out to someone else this week. You'll feel less lonely, and so will the other person. Jesus will be right there with you both.

SUGGESTED HYMNS

- In the Garden
- Nearer My God to Thee
- What a Friend We Have in Jesus

PRAYER REQUESTS AND CLOSING PRAYER

LESSON 9

Sacred Remembrance

KEY VERSE

On my bed I remember you; I think of you through the watches of the night. Because you are my help, I sing in the shadow of your wings. My soul clings to you; your right hand upholds me.
PSALM 63:6–8

OPENING PRAYER

ALMIGHTY GOD, YOU KNOW IT can be difficult for us to remember all that we would like to recall as we get older. But God, we don't ever want to forget to praise You and acknowledge You for Your mercy and love for us. Thank You, Father, for making it possible for us to always remember You. In Jesus' name we pray, amen.

INTRODUCTION

There is a story of three elderly sisters living in the same house. One night the ninety-six-year-old draws a bath, puts her foot in, and pauses. She yells to the other sisters, "Was I getting in or out of the bathtub?" The ninety-four-year-old yells back, "I don't know. I'll come up and see." She starts up the stairs and pauses, then calls out, "Was I going up the stairs or down?" The ninety-two-year-old is sitting at the kitchen table having tea and listening to her sisters. She shakes her head and says, "I sure hope I never get that forgetful, knock on wood," as she raps the table in front of her. She then yells, "I'll come up and help you both as soon as I see who's at the door."

Humor aside, we know that as we grow older, our memories aren't as good as they used to be. Perhaps this is because we have so many things in our minds to remember that some get pushed to the back burners. Whatever the reason, forgetfulness can be aggravating when we try to recall a name or a fact that escapes us.

Experts tell us the brain is like a muscle. Unless we suffer from dementia, our brain grows stronger when we use it. This means we may be better able to remember knowledge stored in our brain once we exercise it. Playing games, working crossword puzzles, learning languages—or even computer programs—all help us keep our brains active and our memory functioning better.

A lecturer in gerontology told her audience, "Don't say you are having a senior moment when you forget something. I have college kids in my classes who leave their homework behind and lose their car keys. Forgetfulness has little to do with age." With that encouragement we simply need to tell ourselves that we can remember that which matters most to us if we work at it. Then we can give ourselves permission to forget all the nonessential information that clutters our minds. Of those truths we store and treasure, none is more important to remember than the knowledge that God is, and was, and always will be. That is a sacred remembrance.

FOR REFLECTION OR DISCUSSION

- Do you have any coping techniques for remembering what you want to remember?
- What sorts of activities are you involved in that exercise your brain?
- To what memories do you cling to most tightly?

SCRIPTURES AND QUOTES

God also said to Moses, "Say to the Israelites, 'The LORD, *the God of your fathers—the God of Abraham, the God of Isaac and the God of Jacob— has sent me to you.' This is my name forever, the name by which I am to be remembered from generation to generation."*
EXODUS 3:15

Remember the wonders he has done, his miracles,
and the judgments he pronounced.
1 CHRONICLES 16:12

Remember to extol his work, which men have praised in song.
JOB 36:24

I will remember the deeds of the LORD; yes, I will remember your miracles
of long ago. I will meditate on all your works and consider all your mighty
deeds. Your ways, O God, are holy. What god is so great as our God?
PSALM 77:11–13

Great are the works of the LORD; they are pondered by all who delight
in them . . . He has caused his wonders to be remembered; the LORD is
gracious and compassionate.
PSALM 111:2, 4

The Lord Jesus, on the night he was betrayed, took bread, and when he
had given thanks, he broke it and said, "This is my body, which is for you;
do this in remembrance of me."
1 CORINTHIANS 11:23–24

Remember Jesus Christ, raised from the dead, descended from David.
2 TIMOTHY 2:8

Remember whose you are and whom you serve. Provoke yourself
by recollection and your affection for God will increase tenfold . . . and
your hope will be inexpressibly bright.[13]
OSWALD CHAMBERS

MEDITATION

Many believers remember the exact moment they asked the Lord
to enter their hearts. Even if the event took place when they were very
small children, the moment of complete surrender, and the joy that
followed it, are permanently etched in their memories.

What could be more sacred to remember than the day we first
believed? The longer we live the more experiences we have stored in
our memory banks. Many of them bring us joy. Some bring us pain
or even regret. But God can mercifully use every memory we have to

mold who we will be in the future—who we will be in His kingdom. This restoration process begins with that first moment of surrender.

Remembering who God is and all He has done for us can be a real joy booster. This knowledge can also build and strengthen our faith to look back over the years and recall the situations in which we know God intervened on our behalf. We garner hope, and the encouragement to pray without ceasing, when we remember all the times God answered our prayers. Usually, such remembrance is also followed by gratitude—even gratitude for the answers we didn't think we wanted to hear, but which turned out to be in our best interest.

Do you ever wonder what memories would sustain you if you were imprisoned in solitary confinement? Have we stored enough if we only have the memories stored in our minds and our hearts to encourage us and keep us sane? How many Bible verses could we recite to ourselves? How many hymns could we sing to boost our morale?

As long as our minds serve us, we need to be filling them with the good news of God's love for us. Those are the sacred remembrances that bring us fulfillment and bring Him glory. Imprisonment is unlikely for most of us, but we may have sleepless nights lying awake in our beds. In those times, sacred remembrances can reassure us, comfort us, and give us hope.

For Reflection or Discussion

- Do you remember the day you first believed in Jesus Christ? How old were you?
- Share memories you have of God's intervention in your life through events or answered prayer.
- Have you memorized any Bible verses? Can you recite them still?

A Thought to Share

God will help us to remember that which honors Him.

Suggestion for the Week

It's never too late to add a sacred remembrance to our memory banks. Select a Bible verse you would like to memorize. Write it out on a piece of paper or card and display it where you will see it every day. Practice saying it until it is yours to keep forever.

Suggested Hymns

- Amazing Grace
- Great Is Thy Faithfulness
- God, Our Help in Ages Past

Prayer Requests and Closing Prayer

Waiting on the Lord

Key Verse

I wait for the LORD, my soul waits, and in his word I put my hope.
Psalm 130:5

Opening Prayer

O Lord, what an impatient people we can be. We aren't good at waiting, Lord. But we know that when we are waiting on You, it's always worth the wait. Give us patience, Lord. Fill us with Your peace as we humbly, expectantly, wait on You to reveal Your glory in this life and the next. In Your Almighty name we pray, amen.

Introduction

Waiting is not one of our favorite things to do, is it? Some days we feel all we do is wait for one thing or another. At breakfast, we wait for our coffee to brew or for our mug to be refilled. During the day we may have to wait for transportation to take us someplace important we need to go, and then we may have to wait in traffic on the way there. Waiting is simply a way of life.

As frustrating as such types of waiting can be, there are periods of waiting we find even more trying. How hard it is to relax when we wait on test results from the doctor or on pain to subside or a depression to lift. It can also be extremely challenging for us when we are waiting to hear from a loved one experiencing an illness or difficult situation. Certainly, the spouses of deployed military men and women know the agony of waiting to learn of their loved one's safe return. Waiting is never easy regardless of the circumstances that have put us temporarily on hold.

And yet any or all these situations can be more bearable when we turn them over to the Lord. When we ask Him to be in control, we know our waiting has a purpose, and He will use it for our good and His. Whatever the circumstances may be, waiting on the Lord is never a waste of our time. He's always worth the wait.

FOR REFLECTION OR DISCUSSION

- What sort of waiting do you find the most difficult to endure?
- Name some times in your life when you are repeatedly asked to wait.
- What emotions does waiting evoke in you?

SCRIPTURES AND QUOTES

I am still confident of this: I will see the goodness of the LORD in the land of the living. Wait for the LORD; be strong and take heart and wait for the LORD.
PSALM 27:13–14

I waited patiently for the LORD; he turned to me and heard my cry.
PSALM 40:1

Yet the Lord longs to be gracious to you; he rises to show you compassion. For the LORD is a God of justice. Blessed are all who wait for him!
ISAIAH 30:18

The Lord is good to those whose hope is in him, to the one who seeks him; it is good to wait quietly for the salvation of the LORD.
LAMENTATIONS 3:25–26

So Christ was sacrificed once to take away the sins of many people; and he will appear a second time, not to bear sin, but to bring salvation to those who are waiting for him.
HEBREWS 9:28

God longs to reveal himself, to fill us with himself. Waiting on God gives
him time in his own way and divine power to come to us.
ANDREW MURRAY

Waiting is not the same as inactivity. Waiting is a commitment to
continue in obedience until God speaks.[14]
PRISCILLA SHIRER

MEDITATION

One of the most treasured accounts in the Bible about waiting is
found in the eleventh chapter of John. Here we read of the death of
Lazarus, a beloved friend of Jesus and brother to Mary and Martha.
The sisters couldn't understand why Jesus lingered so long after
hearing their brother was sick. They waited for Him to come and
work the miracle they knew He was capable of manifesting, but He
didn't come. Instead, their brother died, they buried him in the tomb,
and they began to grieve. After four days, Jesus appeared on the scene!
He said, *"I am the resurrection and the life. He who believes in me will*
live, even though he dies; and whoever lives and believes in me will never
die. Do you believe this?" (John 11:25–26).

The sisters and townsfolk led Jesus to the tomb where Lazarus lay.
As they grieved, Jesus said, *"Did I not tell you that if you believed, you*
would see the glory of God?" (John 11:40). Lazarus emerged from the
tomb alive and was restored to his amazed and grateful sisters. Jesus
used the miracle as a sign to all that He was who He said He was.
Ultimately, the waiting was worth it.

So how about our waiting? How can we make waiting honor
God and open the door to the revelation of His glory as He works
all things together for good in our lives? First, we can acknowledge
He is at work, even when we don't see the evidence of it. We can also
acknowledge that God might be asking us to wait for some reason.
He may be waiting for our situations to change or for our hearts to
undergo a transformation.

Finally, we can give our situation over to Him in prayer, trusting
that once we do, He will put the purpose into our waiting. We can
also enlist others to pray with us so we don't feel so alone. This sort of

active waiting is much easier to bear and opens the door for the Lord to do mighty things.

For Reflection or Discussion

- What's the last situation you remember that required extensive waiting on your part?
- Were you able to give this situation over to God?
- Looking back, can you see how God made the waiting worthwhile? Did He reveal His glory through your situation?

A Thought to Share

Waiting on the Lord is always worth the wait.

Suggestion for the Week

This week be especially aware of situations requiring you to wait. Ask the Lord for patience, and trust He will reveal to you the purpose behind the waiting. Then thank Him and give Him the glory!

Suggested Hymns

- Be Still My Soul
- I Must Tell Jesus
- My Faith Looks Up to Thee

Prayer Requests and Closing Prayer

LESSON 11

Blessed to Be a Blessing

KEY VERSE

I will bless you . . . and you will be a blessing.
GENESIS 12:2

OPENING PRAYER

O LORD, HOW GREATLY YOU BLESS us in ways great and small.
Keep us from overlooking any of Your blessings, Lord. And because
we are people who have been blessed, may we be a blessing to others.
In Jesus' name, amen.

INTRODUCTION

A popular plaque reads, "Thank you, God, for blessing me much
more than I deserve." Most of us upon reading that sentiment would
respond, "Isn't that the truth!"

By definition, we are blessed when we, sometimes unexpectedly,
receive something contributing to our happiness, well-being, or
prosperity. We feel blessed if the weather has been hot and dry and a
gentle rain falls. We feel blessed if someone calls from another state
just to see how we are. Sometimes we may even feel blessed just
because our clothes fit and our shoes match—or because our favorite
pie is on the menu.

We may acknowledge the blessings that come our way or we
may take them for granted. A blessing like a new grandchild, a safer
place to live, or the freedom of religion we enjoy would be hard to

overlook. But do we stop to think about all the "lesser blessings" that are showered upon us? Do we even notice if someone saves us a place at the table or holds a door open as we walk through? If we notice, do we recognize these acts as blessings?

When we do acknowledge our blessings, we may realize they were given to us for a purpose—so we can bless others. Professionals in the field of mental health often tell patients that, when they are feeling down in the dumps, the best cure may be reaching out to help someone else. Many support groups for cancer survivors, widows, parents who have lost a child, and so on, have been started by people who have gone through the same set of circumstances and want to make the difficult experience less painful for others. That's one way we can be a blessing once we ourselves have been blessed.

Of course, we don't have to start a support group to bless others. A blessing can be as simple as passing around a box of chocolates we received as a gift or writing out a Bible verse to encourage someone and slipping it under his or her door.

Each day should be a day to reach out to someone in need for believers in Jesus Christ who know how richly we have been blessed, and who know the Source of all blessings. For we are blessed to be a blessing.

FOR REFLECTION OR DISCUSSION

- What kinds of things might be considered "lesser blessings?"
- When was the last time you felt blessed by, or blessed, someone else?
- Do you differentiate between a blessing and good fortune?

SCRIPTURES AND QUOTES

May those who bless you be blessed!
NUMBERS 24:9

The LORD gives strength to his people;
the LORD blesses his people with peace.
PSALM 29:11

"Bring the whole tithe into the storehouse, that there may be food in my house. Test me in this," says the LORD *Almighty, "and see if I will not throw open the floodgates of heaven and pour out so much blessing that you will not have room enough for it."*
MALACHI 3:10

Give to everyone who asks you, and if anyone takes what belongs to you, do not demand it back. Do to others as you would have them do to you.
LUKE 6:30–31

In everything I did, I showed you that by this kind of hard work we must help the weak, remembering the words the Lord Jesus himself said: "It is more blessed to give than to receive."
ACTS 20:35

Every good and perfect gift is from above, coming down from the Father of the heavenly lights, who does not change like shifting shadows.
JAMES 1:17

You will find, as you look back upon your life, that the moments that stand out, the moments when you have really lived, are the moments when you have done things in a spirit of love.[15]
HENRY DRUMMOND

He who blesses most is blest.
JOHN GREENLEAF WHITTIER

MEDITATION

Our key verse from Genesis 12 is part of God's plan to create a people who would acknowledge Him as the one true God. In its entirety, Genesis 12:2 reads: *"I will make you into a great nation and I will bless you; I will make your name great, and you will be a blessing."* God continues in verse 3: *"I will bless those who bless you, and whoever curses you I will curse; and all peoples on earth will be blessed through you."* He asked Abram, then seventy-five years old, to leave everything he knew, pack up his family, and travel to a faraway land. This was a daunting request, but Abram (later called Abraham) knew that he had to be obedient to receive God's full blessing—for himself and his family and for generations to come.

How about us? Do we miss blessings the Lord intends for us because we aren't obedient to what He asks us to do? If He places certain people on our hearts, do we pick up the phone to encourage them or leave it for another day? If we've been blessed financially, do we share from our wealth to bless those in need? Or do we hoard our money for a rainy day—even though God promises us He will provide? Sharing wealth can include something as close to home as giving money to a family struggling to pay their bills or as widespread as donating to a national ministry that is equipped to change lives all around the globe.

Those of us who believe all blessing comes to us from our Heavenly Father know He is blessing us for a purpose—so we can bless others. Through our faith in Jesus Christ, we have the living water that flows from the very throne of God providing us with an unending supply of blessing. We know we have also received the greatest blessing of all, the gift of eternal life.

As we recall our salvation and all the ways the Lord has blessed us in our lifetime, we can ask Him to show us ways to bless others as we have been blessed. There's no way we can adequately thank the Lord for all the blessings He has given us, but with a grateful heart we can often bless others.

For Reflection or Discussion

- In what ways does God bless us?
- How do we respond to being blessed by Him?
- How could you show God gratitude by blessing someone else as you've been blessed today?

A Thought to Share

We need to be rivers, not lakes. When we are blessed, we must keep the blessing flowing to someone else.

Suggestion for the Week

If someone asks you how you are this week, simply respond with, "I'm more blessed that I deserve." If they ask what you mean, you can share with them the good news of salvation in Jesus Christ. There is no greater blessing to share.

Suggested Hymns

- Come, Thou Fount of Every Blessing
- Count Your Blessings
- Doxology

Prayer Requests and Closing Prayer

LESSON 12

The Solid Rock

KEY VERSE

*The Lord is my rock, my fortress and my deliverer;
my God is my rock, in whom I take refuge.*
PSALM 18:2

OPENING PRAYER

O GOD, HOW WE PRAISE YOU for Your steadfastness. In a world where it can often feel like everything beneath us is sinking sand, you are the Rock on which we stand. Thank You for being our rock and our fortress. In Jesus' name we pray, amen.

INTRODUCTION

A visiting grandmother was walking her grandchildren to school in Charlottesville, Virginia, when she noticed a large red rock in the corner of one of the yards they passed. This particular type of rock was common in Colorado, where she lived, but rarely seen that side of the Mississippi. She and the kids dubbed it the Colorado rock, and the woman secretly hoped that passing it each day would remind her far-away grandchildren that someone in Colorado loved them.

What special rocks are in your memory? Certainly, in school we learned about Plymouth Rock, the traditional site of disembarkation of William Bradford and the Mayflower Pilgrims who founded Plymouth Colony in 1620. It is still visited by tourists to Plymouth, Massachusetts, all these years later. The Rock of Gibraltar, a limestone monolith off the southwestern tip of Europe, is also visited by thousands of tourists yearly, many drawn by a desire to see the nearly three hundred monkeys said to live on its slopes.

Visitors to Jerusalem can't miss seeing the Dome of the Rock which dominates the city skyline. The golden dome was built on the site of the Second Jewish Temple by Muslims to house a rock dubbed "the most contested piece of real estate on earth."[16] This rock has great significance to Jews, Christians, and Muslims. Supposedly it is the rock where Abraham almost sacrificed his son, Isaac, and where the Muslim prophet Mohammad is said to have ascended into heaven—a significant rock indeed.

As famous and well-known as these rocks are, however, eventually they will erode and crumble, or be destroyed. Even though the phrase "solid as the Rock of Gibraltar" was coined to describe someone as resilient as the rock that has withstood many sieges over the years, even that rock will eventually succumb to the ravages of time. Only the rock that is higher than all will survive eternally, and that rock is the Rock of Ages, The Lord Almighty.

FOR REFLECTION OR DISCUSSION

- Have you ever visited one of the famous rocks described above?
- What special rocks are in your memory?
- Have you ever found yourself in sinking sand, only to be saved once you could stand on the rock?

SCRIPTURES AND QUOTES

Trust in the LORD forever, for the LORD, the LORD, is the Rock eternal.
ISAIAH 26:4

So this is what the Sovereign LORD says: "See, I lay a stone in Zion, a tested stone, a precious cornerstone for a sure foundation; the one who trusts will never be dismayed."
ISAIAH 28:16

Therefore everyone who hears these words of mine and puts them into practice is like a wise man who built his house on the rock. The rain came down, the streams rose, and the winds blew and beat against that house; yet it did not fall, because it had its foundation on the rock. But everyone who hears these words of mine and does not put them into practice is like a foolish man who built his house on sand. The rain came down, the streams rose, and the winds blew and beat against that house, and it fell with a great crash.

MATTHEW 7:24–27

For they drank from the spiritual rock that accompanied them, and that rock was Christ.

1 CORINTHIANS 10:4

Consequently, you are no longer foreigners and aliens, but fellow citizens with God's people and members of God's household, built on the foundation of the apostles and prophets, with Christ Jesus himself as the chief cornerstone.

EPHESIANS 2:19–20

As you come to him, the living Stone—rejected by men but chosen by God and precious to him—you also, like living stones, are being built into a spiritual house to be a holy priesthood, offering spiritual sacrifices acceptable to God through Jesus Christ.

1 PETER 2:4–5

It's a good thing to have all the props pulled out from under us occasionally. It gives us some sense of what is rock under our feet and what is sand.[17]

MADELEINE L'ENGLE

The Church's one foundation
Is Jesus Christ her Lord,
She is His new creation
By water and the Word:
From heav'n He came and sought her
To be His holy bride;
With His own blood He bought her
And for her life He died.

SAMUEL J. STONE

Meditation

Most of us have felt like we were standing on quicksand at some point in our lives. No matter what we tried, we weren't able to save ourselves. Instead, we just kept sinking deeper and deeper into the circumstance, the pain, or the grief in which we dwelled. As we age and discover that more aspects of life are out of our control, we can once again feel as if the ground under our feet is less than rock solid.

That's the time we need to plant our feet firmly on the eternal Rock of Ages and to rely fully on God as our rock and our salvation. In the Old Testament, the psalmists often referred to the Lord as their rock and their fortress. Then the prophet Isaiah began to foretell of the coming of the Messiah. Since Jesus is one part of the triune God and completely Divine, He is also our Rock, but in Isaiah and throughout the New Testament He is most often referred to as the Cornerstone—that point on which our faith is built.

So, we sing the words of the old hymn, "My hope is built on nothing less than Jesus' blood and righteousness." Or we clap along to the strains of the old gospel song, "Lead me to the rock that is higher than I." And when we're standing on the Rock, we are higher, aren't we?

The author Hannah Hurnard wrote a Christian allegory about our life journey being a constant climb to be nearer to the Lord and His loving presence. *Hinds' Feet on High Places*, the classic published in 1955, tells the story of Much-Afraid, an everywoman searching for guidance from God to lead her to a higher place. The title comes from Habakkuk 3:19 (KJV): *The LORD God is my strength, and he will make my feet like hinds' feet, and he will make me to walk upon mine high places.* When we are standing on the promises of God, trusting in Him and His Word, we are on solid rock, and we are in a higher place. That's where we want to stand for all eternity.

For Reflection or Discussion

- Why do you think God is called the Rock of Ages?
- What does it mean to you that Jesus is the cornerstone of the Christian faith?
- In what ways has the Lord been your rock and your salvation?

A Thought to Share

We have the peace of the Rock.

Suggestion for the Week

When you encounter others who seem to be walking on sinking sand, introduce them to the Rock of Ages. He will give them a secure place to stand.

Suggested Hymns

- Rock of Ages
- The Church's One Foundation
- The Solid Rock

Prayer Requests and Closing Prayer

LESSON 13

Praying for Perseverance

KEY VERSE

*We also rejoice in our sufferings, because we know that suffering produces
perseverance; perseverance, character; and character, hope.*
ROMANS 5:3–4

OPENING PRAYER

O LORD, HOW DISCOURAGED WE CAN get living out our days on
this earth; how weary we become of holding fast to all that we believe.
Strengthen and empower us, Lord! We don't want to be quitters, but
to persevere in faith until the end. Only with Your help will we be
able to do so. In Jesus' name, amen.

INTRODUCTION

We gain great encouragement from hearing stories about people
who persevere against all odds and eventually reach their goals. Most
of them fall many times along the way, but they simply get up one
more time than they fall. On May 25, 2001, Erik Weihenmayer
became the only blind man in history to reach the summit of the
world's highest peak—Mount Everest. Achieving a feat most sighted
people wouldn't even attempt, he went on to climb all seven of the
highest peaks in the world and has become an inspiration to people
with all kinds of disabilities.

Often failure precedes success in politics, business, science, and
sports. Abraham Lincoln lost several elections before being elected

president of the United States. Walt Disney was fired by a newspaper editor because he "lacked imagination and had no good ideas." Thomas Edison made a thousand unsuccessful attempts at inventing the light bulb. Even the world-famous basketball star Michael Jordan was placed on the junior varsity of his high school basketball team! We know all these people eventually succeeded, but what made the difference? Perseverance.

Similarly, we mustn't give in to the temptation to just give up on life. Maybe we don't have a plan to run for office or invent something. Maybe we aren't planning to climb any mountains or to play professional basketball, but we do have a goal before us. Our goal is to live every single day of our lives in such a way that our life has meaning and brings glory to God. With His help, we can do just that.

FOR REFLECTION OR DISCUSSION

- What failures have you experienced in your lifetime?
- What did you learn from these experiences?
- Looking back, can you see how persevering through a failure eventually led you to the achievement of a goal?

SCRIPTURES AND QUOTES

So do not throw away your confidence; it will be richly rewarded. You need to persevere so that when you have done the will of God, you will receive what he has promised.
HEBREWS 10:35–36

Therefore, since we are surrounded by such a great cloud of witnesses, let us throw off everything that hinders and the sin that so easily entangles, and let us run with perseverance the race marked out for us.
HEBREWS 12:1

Consider it pure joy, my brothers, whenever you face trials of many kinds, because you know that the testing of your faith develops perseverance. Perseverance must finish its work so that you may be mature and complete, not lacking anything.
JAMES 1:2–4

*Blessed is the man who perseveres under trial, because
when he has stood the test, he will receive the crown
of life that God has promised to those who love him.*
JAMES 1:12

*As you know, we consider blessed those who have persevered. You have
heard of Job's perseverance and have seen what the Lord finally brought
about. The Lord is full of compassion and mercy.*
JAMES 5:11

*I know your deeds, your love and faith, your service and perseverance, and
that you are now doing more than you did at first.*
REVELATION 2:19

*God takes the saints like a bow which He stretches and at a certain point
says, 'I can't stand any more,' but God does not heed, He goes on stretching
because He is aiming at His mark, not ours, and the patience of the saints
is that they 'hang in' until God lets the arrow fly.*[18]
OSWALD CHAMBERS

*The words that hurt you, the letter that caused you pain . . . your
financial need—they are all known to Him. He sympathizes as no one
else can and watches to see if through it all, you will dare to trust Him
completely.*[19]
L. B. COWMAN

MEDITATION

Not only do we see examples of people persevering against great
odds in modern-day society, we see them in abundance in God's
Word. The Bible is full of accounts of God's people "hanging in there"
through all kinds of trouble. We most frequently think of the plight
of the Israelites, who spent years as slaves of the Pharaoh followed
by forty years wandering in the desert. Moses was tapped to lead his
people through their trials, and he relied on God's leadership during
all the setbacks that came their way. Although he never entered
the Promised Land, his perseverance, fueled by God's will, made it
possible for the people to do so.

Another inspiring example of perseverance is the story of
Nehemiah. He was in exile in Babylon, yet God put on Nehemiah's

heart a desire to rebuild the wall in Jerusalem. Wisely, Nehemiah first prayed over how to proceed in fulfilling this task. Given permission by the king to make it happen, he traveled to Jerusalem. There he was faced with many obstacles. Enemies attacked the workers. An enormous amount of rubble made the work difficult. Yet, in the end, Nehemiah and the families he recruited to rebuild the wall succeeded. They persevered.

Perseverance can be needed in a physical, emotional, moral, or spiritual sense. Where is God asking you to persevere today? He may not be asking you to wander in the desert or to rebuild a wall around your city, but chances are He has put something on your heart. Like Moses and Nehemiah, accept that you can't do what God asks of you without His strength and intervention. Pray first so the enemy won't succeed in his last-ditch efforts to thwart you. Then you will persevere and succeed.

FOR REFLECTION OR DISCUSSION

- Why is it important to pray before attempting to do what God puts on our hearts to do?
- Where are you being asked to persevere in your life now? What obstacles are you facing?
- Have you asked God to help you overcome the obstacles that keep you from persevering? Why or why not?

A THOUGHT TO SHARE

Prayer provides the power to persevere!

SUGGESTION FOR THE WEEK

Spend some time in prayer and ask God to put something on your heart that you can do for His glory. Then ask for His strength to make it happen.

Suggested Hymns

- Battle Hymn of the Republic
- Onward Christian Soldiers

Prayer Requests and Closing Prayer

Lesson 14

God of All Comfort

Key Verse

Praise be to the God and Father of our Lord Jesus Christ, the Father of compassion and the God of all comfort, who comforts us in all our troubles, so that we can comfort those in any trouble with the comfort we ourselves have received from God.
2 Corinthians 1:3–4

Opening Prayer

O Lord, life hurts sometimes. But we know that when we need salve for our wounds or hope for our hearts, our true comfort comes only and always from You. Comfort us in our distress, Lord, we pray. In Jesus' name, amen.

Introduction

A young woman who had gone through a painful divorce volunteered to be a Bible study mentor at a residential home for single moms and their children. The first time she met the woman whom she was to mentor, she could tell the woman wondered what her mentor-to-be possibly had to offer.

The mentee's countenance changed completely when the young woman shared that she had gone through a divorce and that God had given her restoration through faith in Him and protection for her children while she was a single mother. Now the mentee was open to hearing what her new mentor had to share, and the mentor was able to pass on all the comfort she had received from her Lord and Savior. The young woman then knew that God was redeeming her mistakes to use what she had experienced to comfort someone else.

Isn't that so often the case? We experience a heartache in life, maybe one we aren't sure we'll even survive, but then we see an opportunity to encourage someone else going through a similar situation. In this way, nothing we experience in life is ever wasted. Rather God can turn it into a blessing in the lives of others when we are willing to share our stories with them and encourage them to seek the light in the darkness.

But God can't use our painful journeys and stories if we don't run them past Him first. Realizing our only true comfort and restoration comes from Him, we must humbly come to Him with all the pain and broken pieces of our lives and give all of it to Him. We must come to the foot of the cross and receive His love, His forgiveness, and His healing. Then and only then will we have a story to share that will encourage and comfort someone else.

FOR REFLECTION OR DISCUSSION

- Do you remember a time in your life when someone comforted you by sharing a story from his or her own life?
- How about a time when you were able to share something from your life to comfort someone else?
- Is there anyone you know now who might benefit from hearing about the comfort you've received?

SCRIPTURES AND QUOTES

Give me a sign of your goodness . . .
for you, LORD, have helped me and comforted me.
PSALM 86:17

May your unfailing love be my comfort,
according to your promise to your servant.
PSALM 119:76

> *I lift up my eyes to the hills—*
> *where does my help come from?*
> *My help comes from the* LORD,
> *the Maker of heaven and earth.*
> PSALM 121:1–2

> *Blessed are those who mourn, for they will be comforted.*
> MATTHEW 5:4

> *For just as the sufferings of Christ flow over into our lives, so also through Christ our comfort overflows.*
> 2 CORINTHIANS 1:5

> *May our Lord Jesus Christ himself and God our Father, who loved us and by his grace gave us eternal encouragement and good hope, encourage your hearts and strengthen you in every good deed and word.*
> 2 THESSALONIANS 2:16–17

> *The Lord comforts us, not to make us comfortable, but to make us comforters.*[20]
> JOHN HENRY JOWETT

> *Love comforteth like sunshine after rain.*
> WILLIAM SHAKESPEARE

MEDITATION

During his time on earth Jesus was often found comforting others. He comforted the grieving sisters Mary and Martha when his friend Lazarus died. He calmed the wind, the waves, and the frightened men when a storm raged all around the boat in which He and His disciples were sailing. He calmed the angry crowd and comforted a woman about to be stoned for adultery with only a few words. Such accounts of Jesus as Comforter are scattered throughout the New Testament.

No wonder the disciples were fearful when Jesus told them that the time would come when He would leave them to return to His Father in heaven. But knowing their hearts, He said, *"I will ask the*

Father, and he will give you another Counselor to be with you forever— the Spirit of truth" (John 14:16–17). These earthbound men couldn't fully understand the indwelling of the Holy Spirit until later, but they trusted that what Jesus told them would be true. They would not be left without comfort.

As believers in Jesus Christ, we are blessed to have the Holy Spirit in us to not only comfort us in times of distress or grief, but to guide us toward opportunities to comfort others. He will give us the words when we don't know what to say. When we don't know what to do, we may hear the Spirit whispering, "Just stay close and listen."

At times we may comfort others by reminding them that, in the midst of tragedy and disaster, they can still feel the comforting presence of God. We can speak of God's constant sovereignty and unfailing love and assure those in painful situations that He will be their comfort and strength when all about them seems to be falling apart.

It's never helpful to say to someone who is suffering, "I know just how you feel," because in truth we can never be inside another's head and heart. Yet we can comfort them by sharing a time in our lives when the God of all comfort comforted us by praying with them, by grieving with them, and by leading them to the Lord to receive His comfort through the Holy Spirit.

For Reflection and Discussion

- What stops us from offering others the comfort we ourselves have received?
- Can you remember a time when you know God sent someone to comfort you?
- Was there a time in your life when you were able to comfort someone else by sharing God's love with them?

A Thought to Share

God may permit suffering, but He will also provide comfort.

SUGGESTION FOR THE WEEK

Offer to pray for and with someone you know needing comfort this week. Ask the God of all comfort to give you the words to say. He will.

SUGGESTED HYMNS

- Come, Holy Spirit
- God, Our Help in Ages Past
- The Comforter Has Come

PRAYER REQUESTS AND CLOSING PRAYER

LESSON 15

Never Too Late

KEY VERSE

And everyone who calls on the name of the LORD will be saved.
JOEL 2:32

OPENING PRAYER

O LORD, HOW GRATEFUL WE ARE that anyone who trusts in You at any time can receive the gift of eternal life. Thank you that, as long as we live, it's never too late to walk through the door of Your kingdom into the light of Your love. Help us to reach those who don't yet know You with this truth. In Jesus' name, amen.

INTRODUCTION

Many of us may remember reading *Alice's Adventures in Wonderland*, more commonly shortened to *Alice in Wonderland*, during our younger years—or reading it to our children and grandchildren. In 1865, English author Charles Lutwidge Dodgson wrote the novel under the pen name Lewis Carroll. In the story, a young girl named Alice falls through a rabbit hole into a fantasy world where she meets all sorts of peculiar and interesting characters, the most charming of all being the White Rabbit, who is stressing over being late.

And can't we all relate to his dilemma? What a terrible feeling it is to know we're keeping a friend waiting in a restaurant while we frantically search for our keys or purse. How frustrating to be stuck in traffic when we have tickets to a play, or to wait for a ride that never comes when we hope to be on time for a doctor's appointment.

Unavoidable delays happen, but psychologists tell us that people who are chronically late may have a need to be in control. Even subconsciously they may feel that keeping everyone else waiting will make them seem more important. In truth, whether the delay is intentional or not, waiting for someone past an agreed upon time is annoying. We check the time on our watches. We check our cell phones for a message. And we may have to check our reserve of patience too.

Is that how God feels waiting on those He loves to accept His gift of eternal life? Gratefully, God has an unending supply of patience, but His heart grieves over any of His children who have yet to come to Him in faith. Even so, many keep Him waiting, though they know their days on earth are coming to a close.

For Reflection or Discussion

- Do you tend to be a person who is usually early or late? Why?
- How do you feel when someone keeps you waiting repeatedly?
- Do you ever think of tardiness as a form of disrespect?

Scriptures and Quotes

Seek the Lord while he may be found; call on him while he is near.
Isaiah 55:6

"The time has come," he said. "The kingdom of God is near. Repent and believe the good news!"
Mark 1:15

Then he said, "Jesus, remember me when you come into your kingdom." Jesus answered him, "I tell you the truth, today you will be with me in paradise."
Luke 23:42–43

For since the creation of the world God's invisible qualities—his eternal power and divine nature—have been clearly seen, being understood from what has been made, so that men are without excuse.
ROMANS 1:20

I tell you, now is the time of God's favor, now is the day of salvation.
2 CORINTHIANS 6:2

The one who calls you is faithful and he will do it.
1 THESSALONIANS 5:24

So, as the Holy Spirit says: "Today, if you hear his voice, do not harden your hearts."
HEBREWS 3:7–8

The Lord is not slow in keeping his promise, as some understand slowness. He is patient with you, not wanting anyone to perish, but everyone to come to repentance.
2 PETER 3:9

We never know when our life will come to an end. The time to give your life to Christ is now.[21]
BILLY GRAHAM

MEDITATION

The Bible is full of people who thought they were too old or too sinful to be saved by God's grace or used by Him. God proved them wrong again and again. Think of Moses who adamantly told God he was too old and not well-spoken enough to lead his people out of Egypt. Or Rahab who was a prostitute but who, by faith, hid the Israeli spies in her home and ended up being in the lineage of Christ. Probably both of them thought it was too late for them to be used by God, but it wasn't.

Then there's Zacchaeus, the tax collector whose whole life revolved around cheating other people. Jesus called him down from the tree where he had climbed to get a better view and then went to stay at his house. Then Jesus said, *"Today salvation has come to this house, because this man, too, is a son of Abraham. For the Son of Man came to seek and to save what was lost"* (Luke 19:9–10).

It wasn't too late for any of those people to come to the Lord and accept His gift of eternal salvation through His Son, Jesus Christ, and it's not too late for you. It's not too late for that family member for whom you've prayed for decades, or for the grouchy neighbor living next door to you. God isn't insulted when people who have shunned Him all their lives come to Him at the last minute. Yes, they missed out on a lifetime of walking in His truth, grace, and mercy, but they don't have to spend an eternity separated from Him. Deathbed conversions are real and valid. The thief on the cross believed in Jesus right before he died, and Jesus told him, *"Today you will be with me in paradise"* (Luke 23:43).

As long as we have even one breath left, it's not too late to say yes to the Lord. Today is the day. If you haven't done so, accept Christ as your Lord and Savior. If you have, continue to pray for others, no matter how old or sinful they are, to come to know Him too.

For Reflection and Discussion

- Have you ever told God you were too old to do something He asked you to do? How'd that work out?
- Is there someone in your life for whom you've prayed for many years? Have you been tempted to give up on them?
- What could you do to encourage others that they are not too old or too sinful to be a part of God's family today?

A Thought to Share

If you're sitting on the fence regarding faith in God, make sure you jump down on the right side.

Suggestion for the Week

If you aren't sure that you've given your life to Christ and have the blessed assurance of eternal life, pray this simple prayer: Lord Jesus, I believe you are the Son of God. I confess that I am a sinner in need of salvation. I invite you into my heart to be my Lord and Savior. In Jesus' name, amen.

Suggested Hymns

- Just As I Am
- Pass Me Not
- Jesus Is Calling

Prayer Requests and Closing Prayer

LESSON 16

Breath of God

KEY VERSE

*The LORD God formed the man from the dust of the ground and breathed
into his nostrils the breath of life, and the man became a living being.*
GENESIS 2:7

OPENING PRAYER

FATHER GOD, FORGIVE US FOR going through our days oblivious to
the fact that the very breath in our lungs is a gift from You. Thank You
for this gift of life, Lord. Continue to breathe on us, breath of God. And
may we use the life You give us for Your glory. In Jesus' name, amen.

INTRODUCTION

An older woman looked forward to the programs featuring live
music occasionally held at the assisted living community where she
lived. Often at these events, even though male partners were in short
supply, residents would go out onto the modified dance floor and
dance by themselves or with other residents.

One afternoon dance concert was particularly special because
the woman's daughter was visiting from out of town. "Dance with
me," she said to her surprised daughter, and the two of them swayed
to a wonderful rendition of Louis Armstrong's "What a Wonderful
World," creating a treasured memory for them both.

Afterwards, as they walked down the hall together, the mother
said to her daughter, "I'm going to stop in the nurse's station for
a minute." The daughter waited outside the room, but through

the slightly open door she could see that her mom was receiving treatment with what she called her "puffer," something to alleviate the effects of congestive heart failure brought on by overexertion—like dancing, for instance.

Knowing that her mother had sacrificed her own well-being to create a lasting memory made the dance even more precious to the daughter.

Our ability to breathe normally and comfortably is one of those gifts we can so easily take for granted until it's gone. A head cold can make us stuffy and grumpy because it's difficult to breathe temporarily, but most days we breathe automatically and never give breathing a second thought.

But does God? Does He remember that we are created in His image and that He breathed the gift of life into each one of us? Yes, He does.

FOR REFLECTION OR DISCUSSION

- Do you have, or have you ever had, an illness that makes breathing difficult?
- Have you ever gone scuba diving and used a scuba tank to breathe? Did that make you focus more on each breath?
- Do you now need extra oxygen to help you breathe more easily? If so, how does that make you feel?

SCRIPTURES AND QUOTES

"And to all the beasts of the earth and all the birds of the air and all the creatures that move on the ground—everything that has the breath of life in it—I give every green plant for food." And it was so.
GENESIS 1:30

In his hand is the life of every creature and the breath of all mankind.
JOB 12:10

The Spirit of God has made me; the breath of the Almighty gives me life.
JOB 33:4

Let everything that has breath praise the LORD. Praise the LORD.
PSALM 150:6

Again Jesus said, "Peace be with you! As the Father has sent me, I am sending you." And with that he breathed on them and said, "Receive the Holy Spirit."
JOHN 20:21–22

And he is not served by human hands, as if he needed anything, because he himself gives all men life and breath and everything else.
ACTS 17:25

God's inbreathing into man's nostrils the breath of life called into actual existence his soul.[22]
OSWALD CHAMBERS

MEDITATION

Our lives begin and end with our first and last breaths. An ultrasound of a baby in the womb reveals that the baby's chest expands and contracts. He is in fact breathing, a miracle only God could have engineered, yet he is still dependent on the mother's placenta to act as his lungs. Once the baby is born, if his lungs are fully developed, he takes his first breath on his own and his life apart from his mother begins.

At the end of life, breathing can become increasingly difficult, until ultimately it ceases altogether and the person's life on earth is over. From first breath to last, our lives are in God's hands. The question is, how do we use the gazillion breaths we are given between the first one and the last one? Do we use some of them to share the gospel with someone? Do we use some to sing praises to our most worthy God? Or do we mostly take each breath for granted, never stopping to think that though only God knows how many breaths we've been given, we now have one less.

The scripture verse we read in John 20 is an account of Jesus appearing to His disciples after His resurrection and breathing on them before He sent them out saying, *Receive the Holy Spirit* (v. 22). In doing so, He gave them new life, the same new life given to us when first we believe in Jesus Christ and receive the indwelling of the Holy Spirit. God breathed life into Adam. Jesus breathed new life into the disciples. And all of us have life only because of the breath given us by our Creator.

Jesus knew how He was to spend the breaths He was given while on earth. He healed the sick. He called out to sinners. He ministered to the poor. He preached to the multitudes about God's love, mercy, and grace. As He hung from the cross, having sacrificed Himself to save us from our sins, scripture tells us He *called out with a loud voice, "Father, into your hands I commit my spirit." When he had said this, he breathed his last* (Luke 23:46).

How will you spend the breaths you breathe between now and when you breathe your last? May we all use our breaths wisely and for God's glory.

FOR REFLECTION OR DISCUSSION

- Do you ever wonder how many breaths you have left?
- Can you trust God to give you just the right amount?
- Have you ever praised God for the breath in your lungs? Now is a good time to start.

A THOUGHT TO SHARE

Every breath we take is a gift from God.

SUGGESTION FOR THE WEEK

Find a quiet place this week where you can sit alone and listen to your own breathing. Take several really deep breaths. Praise God as you think about breathing in His love and mercy and breathing out fear and anxiety.

SUGGESTED HYMNS

- Breathe on Me, Breath of God
- Spirit of the Living God

PRAYER REQUESTS AND CLOSING PRAYER

LESSON 17

We Walk in Truth

KEY VERSE

Teach me your way, O LORD, and I will walk in your truth; give me an undivided heart, that I may fear your name.
PSALM 86:11

OPENING PRAYER

LORD, HOW WE RELY ON Your truth to be the guiding light that shows us which way to go. In all seasons of life, Your truth comforts us, corrects us, and gives us direction. Thank you, Lord, for the amazing gift of Your truth in our lives. May we never stray from your truth. In Jesus' name we pray, amen.

INTRODUCTION

From our earliest days, most of us have been taught to tell the truth. We learned at a young age that our lies would always find us out, didn't we? Sometimes the result of not telling the truth was time sitting alone in the corner. At other times, when caught in a lie, we might have even had our mouths washed out with soap. That was one way to learn that lying was bad for us.

As important as it is for us to tell the truth in life, there's another truth that is even more important, and that's God's truth. Denying God's truth about what is right or wrong or what is necessary for us to be saved has more dire circumstances than our youthful fibbing.

Truth or Consequences was a game show popular on the radio in the 1940s and on television for over thirty years, beginning in the 1950s. Players would be asked trivial questions that were impossible to answer, then they had to perform zany acts, or "consequences," much to the delight of the audience. This was all in good fun, and the consequences weren't too serious.

Unfortunately, the consequences of our lack of knowledge of God's truth, or our blatant disregard for it, are serious indeed. While God is compassionate and forgives us for our sins, He is also just and so does not remove the consequences our sins create for us and others. Better to know His truth and walk in it than to suffer the consequences.

For Reflection or Discussion

- Can you remember a time you told a lie when you were a child? What were the consequences?
- Why does disregarding the truth come naturally for us?
- When you consider God's truth, what absolutes come to mind?

Scriptures or Quotes

Test me, O Lord, and try me, examine my heart and my mind; for your love is ever before me, and I walk continually in your truth.
Psalm 26:2–3

For I tell you the truth, many prophets and righteous men longed to see what you see but did not see it, and to hear what you hear but did not hear it.
Matthew 13:17

Then you will know the truth, and the truth will set you free.
John 8:32

This is what we speak, not in words taught us by human wisdom but in words taught by the Spirit, expressing spiritual truths in spiritual words.
1 Corinthians 2:13

If we claim to have fellowship with him yet walk in the darkness, we lie and do not live by the truth. But if we walk in the light, as he is in the light, we have fellowship with one another, and the blood of Jesus, his Son, purifies us from all sin.
1 JOHN 1:6–7

I have no greater joy than to hear that my children are walking in the truth.
3 JOHN 4

Keep one thing forever in view—the truth; and if you do this, though it may seem to lead you away from the opinion of men, it will assuredly conduct you to the throne of God.
HORACE MANN

MEDITATION

We are blessed to serve a God who grants us the great privilege of knowing His truth. Not only did He give us the Holy Bible to outline all the precepts and commandments revealing His absolute truth, but He sent His Son to live among us that we might see truth lived out.

Throughout His ministry, Jesus used stories and parables to teach the truth to the disciples and those who gathered around Him wherever He went. Often, He would begin His teaching by saying, *I tell you the truth* . . . and then go on to reveal one of God's immutable truths by which we are to live. *"I tell you the truth,"* Jesus said in Matthew 17:20, *"if you have faith as small as a mustard seed, you can say to this mountain, 'Move from here to there' and it will move. Nothing will be impossible for you."* In Luke 18:17 Jesus said, *"I tell you the truth, anyone who will not receive the kingdom of God like a little child will never enter it."* Again and again, Jesus speaks truth into darkness: the truth that His Father told Him to speak into a world that disregarded truth at every turn.

Because the Holy Bible is inerrant, without flaw from beginning to end, we can rest in its truth. From the commandments God gave to Moses on the mountaintop to the last words of John in Revelation, God's Word is truth. We can be sure this is true when we read the statement Jesus made in John 14:6, *"I am the way and the truth and the life. No one comes to the Father except through me."*

Truth hurts, we hear when we are young, but the older we grow, the more we know God's truth doesn't hurt. God's truth heals. God's truth gives us the confidence we need to face the future unafraid, for it guarantees that all who believe in Him will be saved. When we walk in God's truth, we are walking in the right direction.

FOR REFLECTION OR DISCUSSION

- What teaching of Jesus means the most to you at this point in your life? Is there a scripture verse you would like to share?
- When you think about God's truth, does it bring you joy or fear?
- Do you believe that God's truth is absolute? Why or why not?

A THOUGHT TO SHARE

It's good to be true to ourselves, but better to be true to God.

SUGGESTION FOR THE WEEK

Can you remember a time when you stretched the truth a bit? If the person to whom you told the mistruth is still around, confess what you did and set the record straight. It will feel so good.

SUGGESTED HYMNS

- Battle Hymn of the Republic
- I Love to Tell the Story

PRAYER REQUESTS AND CLOSING PRAYER

LESSON 18

Being on Mission

KEY VERSE

Therefore go and make disciples of all nations, baptizing them in the name of the Father and of the Son and of the Holy Spirit, and teaching them to obey everything I have commanded you.
MATTHEW 28:19–20

OPENING PRAYER

LORD, WE MAY NOT BE able to go overseas on mission trips as we age, but we want to serve You and do Your kingdom work on earth as long as we live. Help us be aware when You are giving us a mission, Lord, and then help us to fulfill the mission for Your glory. In Jesus' name, amen.

INTRODUCTION

A six-year-old girl approached a police officer who was visiting her school. "Are you a real policeman?" she asked. "Yes, I am," he replied. "Well, my mother told me that if I ever needed help with anything I should go to a police officer," she explained. "That's correct," the officer replied. "How can I help you?" The little girl looked up at the officer and asked, "Will you please tie my shoe?"

Now police officers have a lot of important work to do. They have speeders to stop, bank robbers to wrestle, and criminals to corral. Fortunately, this compassionate police officer knew the most important job he had at that particular time was to bend down and tie the little girl's shoe. He completed the mission that was his to fulfill in that moment.

Can we say the same of ourselves? Do we wake up each day wondering what mission, or assignment, life will bring our way? If we're still breathing, there is something we can do to make life better for those with whom we interact during the day—even if it's just to hold a door for someone or to share a smile with a weary caregiver.

If we start each day with the simple prayer, "Lord, use me," we'll be amazed how many missions the Lord may send us on, even if they all occur right where we live. We are equipped to do what He asks of us because of the spiritual gifts we were given when we first believed and by the indwelling of the powerful Holy Spirit.

With God's help, we can do what He asks of us. Then when we close our eyes at the end of each day, we can think back over when we saw an assignment, or mission, come our way and took the time to complete it to the best of our ability.

For Reflection or Discussion

- Did you ever serve on a mission trip to a distant place? Where did you go and what did you do?
- Do you ever think of doing something nice for someone as being on a mission for God?
- How about the concept of "paying it forward"? Is that something you try to do on a regular basis? Is this your mission?

Scriptures and Quotes

Have I not commanded you? Be strong and courageous. Do not be terrified; do not be discouraged, for the Lord your God will be with you wherever you go."
Joshua 1:9

Then I heard the voice of the Lord saying, "Whom shall I send? And who will go for us?" And I said, "Here am I. Send me!"
Isaiah 6:8

"Come, follow me," Jesus said, "and I will make you fishers of men."
MARK 1:17

Again Jesus said, "Peace be with you! As the Father has sent me, I am sending you."
JOHN 20:21

However, I consider my life worth nothing to me, if only I may finish the race and complete the task the Lord Jesus has given me—the task of testifying to the gospel of God's grace.
ACTS 20:24

We are therefore Christ's ambassadors, as though God were making his appeal through us.
2 CORINTHIANS 5:20

Whatever you do, work at it with all your heart, as working for the Lord, not for men, since you know that you will receive an inheritance from the Lord as a reward.
COLOSSIANS 3:23–24

Have I received a ministry from the Lord? If so, I have to be loyal to it, to count my life precious only for the fulfilling of that ministry.[23]
OSWALD CHAMBERS

MEDITATION

Often we think we aren't worthy of taking on a serious mission for God. A million reasons come to mind as we try to rationalize our reticence to accept an assignment. Maybe we think we're too old, too feeble, too busy, or too tired. Whatever our excuses, and no matter how valid we think they are, God can compensate for our shortcomings with His power, mercy, and grace.

The Bible is full of accounts of times God showed up to help His people complete the mission He presented to them. Through Moses, God sent twelve spies to scout the Promised Land of Canaan. Ten of the twelve returned with reports that the land was inhabited by powerful people and the cities were large and fortified. They thought the Israelites could never take it. But two of the spies, Caleb and

Joshua, said, *"The land we passed through and explored is exceedingly good. If the* LORD *is pleased with us, he will lead us into that land, a land flowing with milk and honey, and will give it to us"* (Numbers 14:7–8). They believed that the Lord would be with them and that the land would be theirs.

Often God stirs a passion within us that results in a mission. Nehemiah was serving in the Babylonian court in Susa when he heard his beloved Jerusalem was in shambles. He got permission to take a leave of absence from his duties and return to Jerusalem to rebuild the wall. Under his leadership, a ragtag group of returned exiles succeeded in rebuilding the wall from the charred rubble (Nehemiah 2–6).

When God gives us an assignment, we may feel the Holy Spirit tapping us on the shoulder. That happened to a woman who learned of a ministry for women whose husbands were in prison. It happened to Jim Rayburn, the founder of Young Life, when his heart went out to teenagers who hadn't had a chance to learn about Jesus, and the same can happen to you.

What breaks your heart? What do you feel passionate about? That may be where God wants you to make a difference—even if your mission is simply to bow your head and pray. And following the Lord's lead will often open up the opportunity to share the good news of the gospel with someone—the greatest mission of all.

FOR REFLECTION OR DISCUSSION

- Is there anything right now that breaks your heart as it breaks God's?
- Do you feel passionate about making a difference in that area?
- What could you do to complete the mission God may be asking you to accept?

A THOUGHT TO SHARE

Being on mission for God means being the hands and feet of Jesus.

Suggestion for the Week

Pay special attention to the small opportunities the Lord may be giving you to be on mission for Him this week. At the end of each day, make note of anything you did in response to His guiding touch.

Suggested Hymns

- Open My Eyes, That I May See
- Take My Life and Let It Be
- Wherever He Leads I'll Go

Prayer Requests and Closing Prayer

LESSON 19

Feeding Our Souls

KEY VERSE

What good will it be for a man if he gains the whole world, yet forfeits his soul? Or what can a man give in exchange for his soul?
MATTHEW 16:26

OPENING PRAYER

O GOD, YOU HAVE GIVEN EACH one of us a soul, and You promise that once we believe in Jesus Christ, Your Son, our souls will live into eternity. Help us to care for our souls here on earth—to keep them well fed and healthy so that we may serve You. In Jesus' name, amen.

INTRODUCTION

We spend a lot of time thinking about the food we put into our bodies. Many of us are blessed to have three meals a day—so three times a day we focus on what we eat and how it may affect us. In times past, we may have simply eaten whatever was put in front of us, but not so today. Today people are encouraged to decide if they will eat meat or be vegetarian or vegan. Menu items claim they are gluten free for those needing that diet choice. Our eggs can come from cage-free chickens and our beef from grass-fed cattle, if we're willing to pay a bit more. Nutritionists apply science to identify people with lactose intolerance and other food allergies.

Gratefully, we now understand more about our food sources and what's really in our food—keeping us from choosing food with harmful hormones or pesticides. Planning meals to avoid specific allergies will make our bodies feel better and be healthier overall. All that is positive, right? But what about our souls? Do we pay as much attention to what we are feeding our souls?

Definitions of what a soul is vary, perhaps because it's difficult to define a spiritual, God-given essence—the immaterial yet very deepest part of us that makes us who we are. God created each of us to have both a body and a soul. Someday our body will wear out and be left behind, but our soul will go on forever.

Given that reality, shouldn't we be feeding our souls well? Shouldn't we take care of our souls even more carefully and intentionally than we care for our bodies? Do we feed our souls despair and discouragement or God's hope, mercy, truth, and grace? It's a question worth exploring.

FOR REFLECTION OR DISCUSSION

- What do you remember about mealtimes in your home when you were growing up?
- Do you have to be careful about what you eat now? Why or why not?
- Have you ever thought about feeding your soul as well as your body?

SCRIPTURES AND QUOTES

Love the LORD your God with all your heart and with all your soul and with all your strength.
DEUTERONOMY 6:5

The LORD is my shepherd, I shall not be in want. He makes me lie down in green pastures, he leads me beside quiet waters, he restores my soul.
PSALM 23:1–3

Why are you downcast, O my soul? Why so disturbed within me? Put your hope in God, for I will yet praise him, my Savior and my God.
PSALM 42:11

Praise the LORD, O my soul; all my inmost being, praise his holy name. Praise the Lord, O my soul, and forget not all his benefits—who forgives all your sins and heals all your diseases, who redeems your life from the pit and crowns you with love and compassion, who satisfies your desires with good things so that your youth is renewed like the eagle's.
PSALM 103:1–5

Listen, listen to me, and eat what is good, and your soul will delight in the richest of fare.
ISAIAH 55:2

This is what the LORD says: "Stand at the crossroads and look; ask for the ancient paths, ask where the good way is, and walk in it, and you will find rest for your souls."
JEREMIAH 6:16

Finally, brothers, whatever is true, whatever is noble, whatever is right, whatever is pure, whatever is lovely, whatever is admirable—if anything is excellent or praiseworthy—think about such things.
PHILIPPIANS 4:8

Dear friend, I pray that you may enjoy good health and that all may go well with you, even as your soul is getting along well.
3 JOHN 2

Hide me, O my Savior, hide, till the storm of life is past; safe into the haven glide, O receive my soul at last.
CHARLES WESLEY

MEDITATION

In his book, *Soul Keeping: Caring for the Most Important Part of You*, author and pastor John Ortberg wrote, "We all have two worlds, an outer world that is visible and public and obvious, and an inner world that may be chaotic and dark or may be gloriously beautiful. In the end, the outer world fades. We are left with the inner world. It is what we will take with us. I am an unceasing spiritual being with an eternal destiny in God's glorious universe."[24]

The inner world we have is our soul, but we aren't bodies with a soul. In truth, we are souls with temporary bodies. When people see us, they initially see our bodies, but since the eyes are the window to the soul, maybe they can catch a glimpse of our souls as well.

If you pass someone in the hall with downcast eyes and a defeated posture, aren't you seeing the condition of his or her soul? If the next person you pass greets you with a smile and you see the light of the love of Jesus in his or her eyes, aren't you then seeing a bit of a healthier soul?

Our souls can take a beating as we journey through life. Disappointments, tragedies, deep losses affect us all. Yet a soul fed a steady diet of God's truth is well grounded and can remain strong no matter what. After the loss of all four of his daughters in a storm at sea in November 1873, Horatio Spafford looked out over the vast ocean where they perished and penned the words to one of our most beautiful hymns, "It Is Well with My Soul." He could never have given us those words unless his soul was well fed and prepared to sustain him through his heartbreaking loss.

What's the condition of our souls? How can we feed our souls? Nothing we eat or drink will give us a well-fed soul. Watching too much TV can be like feeding our souls junk food. We feed our souls when we open God's Word, when we praise God for a sunrise, when we forgive one another, or pray with a grateful heart. Can we say, "It is well with my soul," or do we have more care and feeding to do— more scripture reading, more prayer, more praise to restore our souls and make them glow with the light of Jesus? It's never too late to feed our souls.

For Reflection or Discussion

- Have you ever said of someone, "Oh, what a beautiful soul!" What inspired you to say that?
- Who do you know now who seems to have a healthy soul shining from his or her eyes?
- What could you do to feed your soul today?

A Thought to Share

Whatever is good for your soul, do that.

Suggestion for the Week

No matter what troubles come your way this week, take a deep breath and say, "It is well with my soul."

Suggested Hymns

- It Is Well (Bethel Music)
- It Is Well with My Soul
- Jesus, Lover of My Soul

Prayer Requests and Closing Prayer

LESSON 20

When God Speaks

KEY VERSE

I will walk among you and be your God, and you will be my people.
LEVITICUS 26:12

OPENING PRAYER

LORD GOD, HOW WE LONG to hear Your voice. How we hold fast to every word You speak to us through Your holy Scripture. Open our ears and our hearts to everything You want to say to us, Lord. We trust You, and we want to hear from You. In Jesus' name, amen.

INTRODUCTION

Before we accept information as truth, it's wise to consider the source, isn't it? For years people have lamented, "You can't believe everything you read in the papers," and that's never been more true than it is now with the unfortunate demise of objective truth in journalism. We may think we've discovered a reliable source for news only to learn the truth was edited or distorted by that source too. Once we lose trust, it's hard to get it back.

Likewise, if a friend or relative tells us something, we immediately run what is said through the filter of our past experiences with this person. Has this friend or relative always been truthful with us, or do they have a propensity for stretching the truth a bit, or for exaggerating to the point of destroying the truth all together? When someone we know is prone to gossip, we take everything they tell us with a grain of salt. We might follow up with a question such as,

"Who told you that?" or "How do you know?" It's important for us to establish credibility and find out if our source can be trusted.

So, who can we always trust? Whose words, whether spoken or written, are pure gold and can be relied on to convey the immutable truth? Only those which come from the Lord. We can trust everything He says to us because His credentials are impeccable, and He can never lie. Hold fast to the commandments and promises of the Lord God Almighty, and you will never be misinformed, disillusioned, or disappointed.

For Reflection or Discussion

- Do you have a source of information that you trust without a doubt?
- Have you ever been taken in by a mistruth from someone?
- How can we keep ourselves from gossiping or spreading lies?

Scriptures and Quotes

For this is what the LORD says—he who created the heavens, he is God; he who fashioned and made the earth, he founded it; he did not create it to be empty, but formed it to be inhabited—he says: "I am the LORD, and there is no other."
ISAIAH 45:18

"As for me, this is my covenant with them," says the LORD. "My Spirit, who is on you, and my words that I have put in your mouth will not depart from your mouth, or from the mouths of your children, or from the mouths of their descendants from this time on and forever," says the LORD.
ISAIAH 59:21

This is what the LORD says: "Restrain your voice from weeping and your eyes from tears, for your work will be rewarded," declares the LORD.
JEREMIAH 31:16

It is written: " 'As surely as I live,' says the Lord, 'every knee will bow before me; every tongue will confess to God.' "
ROMANS 14:11

I will be a Father to you, and you will be my sons and daughters,
says the Lord Almighty.
2 CORINTHIANS 6:18

"I am the Alpha and the Omega," says the Lord God,
"who is, and who was, and who is to come, the Almighty."
REVELATION 1:8

Blessed be God's voice, for it is true,
and falsehoods have to cease before it!
THOMAS CARLYLE

People are meant to live in an ongoing conversation
with God, speaking and being spoken to.[25]
DALLAS WILLARD

MEDITATION

Throughout the Old Testament, God spoke audibly to people who needed His direction to fulfill His will. We read of His conversations with Abraham, Noah, and all the Old Testament prophets as He communicated clearly and directly with His people through them. Consider all the conversations God had with Moses. He told Moses to go to Pharaoh and demand that he let the Israelites go from the bondage of slavery. He told Moses to trust Him and lead all those people into the Red Sea—and that turned out well! When He gave Moses the Ten Commandments on Mount Sinai, He was speaking not only to Moses, but to His people for all generations. He was speaking to us (Exodus 20:1–17).

There are those who may say that once the Messiah, Jesus Christ, arrived, the Ten Commandments were no longer relevant. Not so. God's guidance for how we are to be in relationship with Him and with others is as relevant today as when His words were first inscribed on those tablets by His own hand. Our mission, through prayer and discernment, is to see how clearly the Ten Commandments relate to our culture today. To see how He is speaking truth into our lives now.

Yet we have so much more than the Ten Commandments to live by. As we read the Bible, we hear God speaking to us on every page. His promises are true and as good as gold. His admonitions are for our benefit. His expressions of love, mercy, grace, and hope are life-giving, today and throughout eternity. When God speaks, we can believe what He says.

We may not hear the audible voice of God often or ever, but that doesn't mean He has stopped speaking to His people. He speaks to us through the Holy Spirit that indwells us—sending messages into our hearts, minds, and souls that we discern as coming only from Him. He speaks to us in response to our heartfelt prayers, through conversations with other believers, and through circumstances in which we clearly see His hand at work. And always, always, He continues to speak to us through His living Word, the Holy Bible.

To hear God clearly, we must be in a loving relationship with Him. Then and only then can we be sure it is Him speaking to us. When God speaks, it is a gift to us. Once we hear Him, regardless of our stage of life or circumstances, we will be blessed if we listen and respond in faith.

FOR REFLECTION OR DISCUSSION

- To review, in what ways does God speak to us today?
- Have you heard God speak to you? How?
- How can we know it is God who is speaking?

A THOUGHT TO SHARE

When God speaks, we should listen,
knowing that when God speaks, things happen.

SUGGESTION FOR THE WEEK

Keep a list of anything you believe God is saying to you at this stage of your life. Remember He may speak to you through the Holy Spirit, through His Word, through other people, through answers to prayer, or through your circumstances.

Suggested Hymns

- He Lives
- In the Garden
- Standing on the Promises

Prayer Requests and Closing Prayer

LESSON 21

Living in the Light

KEY VERSE

God is light; in him there is no darkness at all.
1 JOHN 1:5

OPENING PRAYER

LORD GOD, YOU TRULY DO light up our lives with Your love, mercy, truth, and grace. Protect us from the darkness that tries to envelop us and keep us living as children of the light, we pray. In Jesus' name, amen.

INTRODUCTION

In a craggy canyon near Manitou Springs, Colorado, is a well-visited tourist site called The Cave of the Winds. First discovered by two adventurous, young brothers in 1881, the cave is really an underground wonderland of various caverns covered with stalactites and stalagmites.

Thousands of tourists and a multitude of school children on field trips trek through this cave each year. All can later recall the point on the tour when the guide extinguishes all the lights and they are plunged into complete, all-encompassing darkness. After just a few moments for the group to completely experience how it feels to be surrounded by pitch black, the guide flicks a light switch or lights a kerosene lantern (depending on which tour is chosen) and the walls of the cave, the stalactites, and the stalagmites are visible once again.

Maybe we haven't all been in the deep, dark depths of a cave, but we all can relate to what a relief it is to light a candle when the power goes off in a storm or even to have a nightlight in an unfamiliar hotel room. Light keeps us safe. Light is life-giving. Light separates night from day. We need light.

The Bible returns to the theme of light versus darkness frequently. In scripture, light usually represents good, righteousness, and truth—while darkness represents evil, wickedness, and deception. As we read above, 1 John 1:5 tells us that, in fact, *God is light; in him there is no darkness at all.* Why would we ever want to dwell in darkness when we could live in the light God provides? Let's live in the light.

For Reflection or Discussion

- Have you ever been in a cave where you were in total darkness? What was that like?
- Can you think of a time in your life when you were in desperate need of some source of light?
- Why do you think the Bible talks about light versus darkness so much?

Scriptures and Quotes

You, O Lord, keep my lamp burning;
my God turns my darkness into light.
Psalm 18:28

The Lord is my light and my salvation—whom shall I fear?
Psalm 27:1

Let us walk in the light of the Lord.
Isaiah 2:5

You are the light of the world . . . let your light shine before men, that they may see your good deeds and praise your Father in heaven.
Matthew 5:14, 16

The light shines in the darkness, but the darkness has not understood it.
John 1:5

*Ye are all the children of light, and the children of the day:
we are not of the night, nor of darkness.*
1 Thessalonians 5:5 (KJV)

But you are a chosen people, a royal priesthood, a holy nation, a people belonging to God, that you may declare the praises of him who called you out of darkness into his wonderful light.
1 Peter 2:9

But if we walk in the light, as he is in the light, we have fellowship with one another, and the blood of Jesus, his Son, purifies us from all sin.
1 John 1:7

There will be no more night. They will not need the light of a lamp or the light of the sun, for the Lord God will give them light.
Revelation 22:5

Our light is to shine in the darkness; it is not needed in the light.[26]
Oswald Chambers

Meditation

Often you can see the light of Jesus Christ's love shining from people's eyes when they believe in Him and have a close relationship with Him. Wherever they go, they take His light with them. And isn't that light always needed? At the bedside of a sick friend, His light brings comfort. When we are with someone who is grieving, His light brings hope. Even if as believers we experience the loneliness of a dark night, His light reminds us that He will always be with us.

Those who are open to a relationship with Jesus Christ are drawn toward His light when they see it in someone else, while those who have chosen to reject Him are repulsed. In John 3:20–21 Jesus says, *"Everyone who does evil hates the light, and will not come into the light for fear that his deeds will be exposed. But whoever lives by the truth comes into the light, so that it may be seen plainly that what he has done has been done through God."* Have you ever tried to make friends with those who seem to go out of their way to avoid you? Don't take it personally. It may be that they see the light of Jesus you are offering them, and they are not yet ready to receive it.

Yet should their response change our attitude toward others? Not at all. The Bible encourages believers to share the light they have wherever they go, not keep it *under a bushel* (Matthew 5:15 KJV). The Bible also warns us not to be yoked together with unbelievers because *what fellowship can light have with darkness?* (2 Corinthians 6:14). We are to share the light but avoid the darkness.

How are we to respond to all this teaching about light versus darkness in the Bible? First, we need to believe in Jesus Christ so we will be indwelled by the Holy Spirit. Then His light will be with us wherever we go. The closer we grow in relationship to Him, the more likely it will be that someone will see His light shining from our eyes and be drawn to Him. Live in the light, and others may want to do so too.

For Reflection or Discussion

- Have you ever met someone who seemed to have the light of the Lord shining from their eyes? Please share.
- Has anyone ever told you that they see the Lord in you? How did that make you feel?
- What difference does it make in our lives if we are living in the light?

A Thought to Share

When you shine the light of the Lord, no batteries are required!

Suggestion for the Week

Sit in total darkness and ask the Lord to shine His light into your life anew. Then strike a match or flip a switch and let the light you see remind you that you can bask in His light.

Suggested Hymns

- Immortal, Invisible
- This Little Light of Mine
- Thy Word

Prayer Requests and Closing Prayer

LESSON 22

The Lord's Gentle Touch

KEY VERSE

*After the earthquake came a fire, but the LORD was not in the fire.
And after the fire came a gentle whisper.*
1 KINGS 19:12

OPENING PRAYER

LORD GOD, WE PRAISE YOU for Your awesome power, strength, and majesty, but we also praise You for those times when You are gentle with us. Keep us safe in Your kind and gentle hands, we pray. In Jesus' name, amen.

INTRODUCTION

We see the gentleness in the caress of a mother as she cuddles her newborn or receive the gentle touch of a friend's hand on our shoulder, and we are blessed. We know gentleness makes our world better, but are we ourselves doing enough to spread such gentleness?

While gentle behavior is defined as meekness and humility, it takes courage and strength for us to be gentle and to move through the world gently. Gentleness requires humility. This means not thinking less of ourselves but thinking of ourselves less. Humility means giving up the idea we always have to be the best, the most, the wisest, or the one who's always right. Humility might even mean sacrificing our desire so we can satisfy someone else's. When we behave gently, we reflect humility, which is a difficult trait for many.

The term "horse whisperer" became part of our culture's vernacular after Robert Redford's 1998 movie *The Horse Whisperer*. This procedure involves techniques such as eye contact and body language used to train horses in a gentler, more humane way than the former practice of riding or beating them into submission. Now anyone who takes a gentle approach with an animal may be dubbed a "dog whisperer" or "cat whisperer" for instance.

What's true with animals is also true of humans. We are more likely to engage with someone who is gentle with us. We are more willing to drop our defenses and develop a mutually beneficial relationship of respect and trust with a gentle person. Maybe we should all become "people whisperers."

We don't have to look far for a role model if our goal is to be gentler. Even though Jesus had all the power of the universe at His command, He almost always moved gently through the world. Referring to Himself as the Good Shepherd. Receiving small children and blessing them. Gently touching the eyes of a blind man. If we would be gentler, we should follow the example set by the gentle Son of Man.

FOR REFLECTION OR DISCUSSION

- What do you think of, even in the natural world, when you hear the word *gentle*?
- When was the last time someone was gentle with you?
- Do you consider gentleness an important attribute? Why or why not?

SCRIPTURES AND QUOTES

He tends his flock like a shepherd: He gathers the lambs in his arms and carries them close to his heart; he gently leads those who have young.
ISAIAH 40:11

Rejoice greatly, O Daughter of Zion! Shout, Daughter of Jerusalem! See, your king comes to you, righteous and having salvation, gentle and riding on a donkey, on a colt, the foal of a donkey.
ZECHARIAH 9:9

*Come to me, all you who are weary and burdened, and I will give you
rest. Take my yoke upon you and learn from me, for I am gentle and
humble in heart, and you will find rest for your souls. For my yoke is easy,
and my burden is light.*
MATTHEW 11:28–29

*But the fruit of the Spirit is love, joy, peace, patience,
kindness, goodness, faithfulness, gentleness and self-control.
Against such things there is no law.*
GALATIANS 5:22–23

*Be completely humble and gentle;
be patient, bearing with one another in love.*
EPHESIANS 4:2

*Therefore, as God's chosen people, holy and dearly loved, clothe yourselves
with compassion, kindness, humility, gentleness and patience.*
COLOSSIANS 3:12

*Your beauty should not come from outward adornment, such as braided
hair and the wearing of gold jewelry and fine clothes. Instead, it should
be that of your inner self, the unfading beauty of a gentle and quiet spirit,
which is of great worth in God's sight.*
1 PETER 3:3–4

Nothing is so strong as gentleness, nothing so gentle as real strength.
FRANCIS DE SALES

*It is only imperfection that complains of what is imperfect.
The more perfect we are, the more gentle and quiet
we become towards the defects of others.*[27]
FRANÇOIS FÉNELON

MEDITATION

Gentleness is listed as part of the fruit of the Spirit in Galatians
5:22–23, yet some people call gentleness the forgotten fruit. It
seems to come more naturally for us to exhibit joy, kindness, even
patience than it is for us to approach a situation or relationship with
gentleness.

Yet as believers in Jesus Christ we have the indwelling of the Holy Spirit to give us the power we need to set aside our pride and be humble and gentle with others if we ask for His help in doing so. While spiritual gifts vary from one believer to the next, we all have the fruit of the Spirit to draw on.

The book of Proverbs in the Bible contains an important reminder about the virtue of gentleness. *A gentle answer turns away wrath, but a harsh word stirs up anger* (Proverbs 15:1). We don't often think about being gentle with our response when a contentious situation or argument confronts us. Yet a gentle approach can diffuse the situation quickly. The Bible says so.

Perhaps the most important reason for cultivating gentleness in our daily walk is that, as with the horse whisperer, our gentleness will draw others closer to us. Theologian Dallas Willard called this "the allure of gentleness." Once people feel safe in our presence, we can share with them the truth of the gospel, and they will be better able to receive it.

We read in 1 Peter 3:15, *But in your hearts set apart Christ as Lord. Always be prepared to give an answer to everyone who asks you to give the reason for the hope that you have. But do this with gentleness and respect.* How will people know we have the hope of eternal life through salvation in Jesus Christ if they can't get close enough to us to find out? Hitting them over the head with the truth of the gospel message is seldom effective. Gently sharing what we believe and why is.

Knowing we have access to all the gentleness we need should encourage us to pray for more gentleness in our lives. After all, gentleness begets gentleness, and we could all use more.

For Reflection or Discussion

- Why do you think it's difficult for us to respond to people with gentleness?
- When has a gentle response from another made a difference in your life?
- Have you ever gently shared the message of salvation with someone? How did that go?

A Thought to Share

It can be hard to be gentle, but gentleness softens hardness.

Suggestion for the Week

If you find yourself in a difficult conversation with someone this week, pray silently for more gentleness as you respond. The Lord will provide.

Suggested Hymns

- He Touched Me
- Softly and Tenderly

Prayer Requests and Closing Prayer

LESSON 23

Living a Life Worthy

KEY VERSE

*As a prisoner for the Lord, then, I urge you to
live a life worthy of the calling you have received.*
EPHESIANS 4:1

OPENING PRAYER

O LORD, LIFE CAN SEEM SO meaningless to us sometimes. Yet
You promise that we can live productive lives, drawing ourselves and
others closer to You until the day we die. Be our life coach, Lord.
Patiently reveal to us how we can live a life worthy of the calling You
gave us. In Your precious name we pray, amen.

INTRODUCTION

Sometimes we dedicate several hours to watching a television
show only to click the off button with a disgruntled comment like,
"Well, that was not worthy of my time." Why do we feel like this?
Probably because we know we aren't better people for having spent
our time in that way—we're no smarter, no more informed about how
to navigate life, and maybe we aren't even entertained if the program
was really bad. A good nap might have been more beneficial.

So, what is worthy of our time? Visiting a friend who is feeling
down would be a fulfilling use of an hour or two. Exercising to keep
our bodies strong, reading a good novel or a riveting biography,
tending to plants, animals—and grandchildren. We could list a

hundred worthy uses of our time if we really stop to think about what we are doing instead of just mindlessly watching whatever appears on the television in front of us.

What makes the difference between an activity that is worthy, and one that is simply a waste of time? A dictionary definition of worthy is "having worth, merit, or value; useful or valuable." If activities aren't labeled worthy, then they may be the opposite—worthless. Unfortunately, people can be labeled worthy or worthless, too. There's nothing worthless about any of us, however, because we are all created in the image of God.

People of any age can suffer from feelings of unworthiness. Life has a way of pelting us with disappointments, and other people have a way of damaging or distorting our concept of our self-worth if we listen to the wrong messages often enough to believe them. In truth, only God is worthy. But when we believe we can be worthy because He is worthy, then it is possible for us to live, as Paul said, "a life worthy of the calling" (Ephesians 4:1).

For Reflection or Discussion

- What's the last thing you did that felt like a worthless waste of time?
- How did that realization make you feel?
- Could you do anything to redeem the time you wasted?

Scriptures and Quotes

> *"I call to the LORD, who is worthy of praise,*
> *and I am saved from my enemies."*
> 2 SAMUEL 22:4

> *For great is the LORD and most worthy of praise;*
> *he is to be feared above all gods.*
> 1 CHRONICLES 16:25

> *Great is the LORD and most worthy of praise;*
> *his greatness no one can fathom.*
> PSALM 145:3

Anyone who does not take his cross and follow me is not worthy of me.
MATTHEW 10:38

He is the one who comes after me, the thongs of whose
sandals I am not worthy to untie.
JOHN 1:27

For this reason, since the day we heard about you, we have not stopped
praying for you and asking God to fill you with the knowledge of his will
through all spiritual wisdom and understanding. And we pray this in
order that you may live a life worthy of the Lord and may please him in
every way: bearing fruit in every good work, growing in the knowledge of
God, being strengthened with all power according to his glorious might
so that you may have great endurance and patience, and joyfully giving
thanks to the Father, who has qualified you to share in the inheritance of
the saints in the kingdom of light.
COLOSSIANS 1:9–12

In a loud voice they sang: "Worthy is the Lamb,
who was slain, to receive power and wealth and wisdom
and strength and honor and glory and praise!"
REVELATION 5:12

True happiness . . . is not attained through self-gratification but through
fidelity to a worthy purpose.[28]
HELEN KELLER

The longer you live the more you discover that "Just because you're
breathing doesn't mean you're living." From God's point of view, breathing
does not equal life.[29]
RON R. RITCHIE

MEDITATION

What if the only part of your life with any lasting value is the part
you don't really live at all? What if it's only in those times when you
allow Jesus Christ to live His life through you that you are living what
is described as "a life worthy" in both Ephesians 4:1–3 and Colossians
1:9–12? Because believers have the Holy Spirit living in them, with
all the gifting and power that implies, our job is merely to get out of

the way so Christ can live through us. Then, and only then, will we be able to live a life worthy of the calling to love God, to love others, and to serve Christ.

In the Ephesians passage, living a life worthy is described as one lived out in humility, gentleness, love, unity, and peace. The Colossians passage includes pleasing God in every way, bearing fruit in every good work, and exhibiting knowledge of God, strength, endurance, patience, and gratitude. Given that list of attributes, is it any wonder none of us feels as if we are living the life God asks us to live?

Yet the good news is that while we don't live in such a worthy way every moment of every day, we get glimpses of that worthy life whenever we take the time to encourage another, share the good news of the gospel, or reach out in love and gentleness to those around us. We may even feel the Lord's pleasure at those times.

It's only normal for even Christians to feel worthless occasionally, but we must never forget that in God's eyes we are worthy. Worthy of being the hands and feet of Jesus as we travel down our life's path, wherever it takes us today. Worthy to be sons and daughters of the King of Kings. Worthy to hold our heads high and be assured that no matter what anyone says about us or does to us, we are worthy of eternal life with our King because He lived a life worthy among us and then died for our sins.

Whatever earthly life we have left, let's fill it with moments of holy worthiness—doing small acts of kindness, saying thank you for each sunrise and sunset, being patient in times of trial. God gives us the power to do all that and more, and when we do, it makes Him smile.

FOR REFLECTION OR DISCUSSION

- Recall a time when you knew you were living a life worthy of your call as a believer in Jesus Christ. You may have been engaged in something very small in your eyes but very large in God's.
- How did that make you feel at the time?
- Who comes to mind who seems to be living "a life worthy" most of the time?

A Thought to Share

We can't change the past or predict the future, but we can live a worthy life in this present moment.

Suggestion for the Week

Keep a daily log this week of how you spend your time. At the end of each day, put a star by any activity indicating you are living "a life worthy."

Suggested Hymns

- Holy, Holy, Holy
- Take My Life and Let It Be
- Worthy Is the Lamb

Prayer Requests and Closing Prayer

LESSON 24

Forgiveness Is Forever

KEY VERSE

Be kind and compassionate to one another, forgiving each other,
just as in Christ God forgave you.
EPHESIANS 4:32

OPENING PRAYER

LORD JESUS, WE KNOW YOU forgave everyone who wronged You during Your time on earth, but it can be so hard for us, Lord. Please open our hearts and minds to the healing and peace forgiveness can bring. In Your name we pray, amen.

INTRODUCTION

Two little boys in the same neighborhood quarreled. But the next morning, Luke grabbed his football and headed for Ben's house again. Surprised, his mom asked teasingly, "What? You're going to play with Ben? You said yesterday you weren't ever going to play with him again. Don't you remember?"

Luke looked a little sheepish, dug his toe into the carpet for a moment, then flashed a satisfied smile as he hurried away. "Oh, Ben and me's good forgetters," he called out, the screen door slamming behind him.

We need to learn to be "good forgetters" if we are to truly forgive people with whom we have a disagreement. It's easy to get into the habit of holding a grudge instead, of becoming what some have labeled "gunny sackers," stashing away one offense after another in our emotional gunny sacks. Then the next time we have a disagreement with the same person we can dump all our grievances out on them at one time. That's not the best approach to restoration and forgiveness in a relationship though, is it?

Forgiveness is only complete once we have forgotten the offense. As we age, we may find forgiving people who wronged us this morning easier than forgiving someone who offended us decades ago. That's because long-term memory stays intact longer. But any offense we can recall must be forgiven if we are to be free of the bondage of it.

Unforgiveness can even affect our overall health. In fact, it's been said not forgiving someone is like drinking poison and waiting for the other person to die. Studies have shown that a failure to forgive can affect our blood pressure and heart rate and lead to different kinds of pain and depression. We will benefit if we forgive anything we are still holding against another person—whether they ask for our forgiveness or not. But the best reason of all for us to forgive is because God forgives us—and asks us to do the same for others.

For Reflection or Discussion

- Can you think of any grudges you are harboring from the past?
- What would it take for you to be able to let those go?
- Is there anything for which you have not forgiven yourself?

Scriptures and Quotes

For as high as the heavens are above the earth, so great is his love for those who fear him; as far as the east is from the west, so far has he removed our transgressions from us.
Psalm 103:11–12

If you, O Lord, kept a record of sins, O Lord, who could stand? But with you there is forgiveness; therefore you are feared.
Psalm 130:3–4

*For I will forgive their wickedness and will
remember their sins no more.*
JEREMIAH 31:34

*For if you forgive men when they sin against you, your heavenly Father
will also forgive you. But if you do not forgive men their sins, your Father
will not forgive your sins.*
MATTHEW 6:14–15

Father, forgive them, for they do not know what they are doing.
LUKE 23:34

*All the prophets testify about him that everyone who believes in him
receives forgiveness of sins through his name.*
ACTS 10:43

*Bear with each other and forgive whatever grievances you may have
against one another. Forgive as the Lord forgave you.*
COLOSSIANS 3:13

*None of us is God, but we can all reflect Him when we are able to forgive
as He forgave us, giving His Son to die for our sins.*[30]
HENRI J. M. NOUWEN

MEDITATION

As Jesus walked this earth, He experienced everything the human condition brings, just so He could be our high priest in all ways, and so we could come to Him with anything that threatens our peace. As we may also, He experienced betrayal from those closest to Him. Yet He called Judas Iscariot a friend until the end. Although Peter denied Him three times, Jesus made sure Peter was informed that He had risen from the grave (Mark 16:5–7), and then gave him three chances to proclaim His love for Him to negate the three denials (John 21:15–17).

Yes, Jesus modeled perfect forgiveness, even asking His Father to forgive those who crucified Him, *"for they do not know what they are doing"* (Luke 23:34). He died for our sins so we can be completely forgiven and dwell with Him in eternity.

We aren't Jesus. Forgiveness can be more difficult for us. But we can forgive those who wronged us or disappointed us by drawing on His grace, mercy, and love.

The cost of not forgiving is high. Not only can an old grudge eat away at the person holding on to the negative feeling, but a grudge can also affect future generations once that person passes away. Family feuds lasting for generations often begin with one person refusing to forgive another family member for a wrong committed. Wouldn't we all rather leave a legacy of forgiveness than one of anger and animosity that could negatively impact descendants we won't even meet? Making peace with the past before *we* pass leaves a future free of the pain of unforgiveness to those who follow us.

A statement of blanket forgiveness can be helpful if it seems too late, or too painful, to work through differences in detail. Consider saying to a friend, or even to an adult child, "I know we haven't always been all we could have been to one another, but I forgive you, and I hope you can forgive me."

Through the power of the Holy Spirit, we can forgive past grievances, even if the person we need to forgive has never asked for our forgiveness or is no longer living. The weight of bitterness or resentment can be lifted from our shoulders. Once we forgive, we must pray we can be "good forgetters" and completely forget the offense. Then forgiveness is forever.

For Reflection or Discussion

- Why do you think it's so difficult for us to forgive others, even when forgiveness is necessary?
- Writing a simple note or making a phone call can open the door to forgiveness. Have you ever received or sent such a message of reconciliation?
- As you've listened to this lesson, has anyone come to mind whom you need to forgive? Consider doing so now in your heart.

A Thought to Share

Forgiveness is a gift we give ourselves.

Suggestion for the Week

Choose forgiveness. While anger and resentment are common responses, do the hard work of choosing forgiveness instead. Ask Jesus to help you.

Suggested Hymns

- Jesus Paid It All
- Nothing but the Blood of Jesus

Prayer Requests and Closing Prayer

LESSON 25

Be Happy

KEY VERSE

But may the righteous be glad and rejoice before God;
may they be happy and joyful.
PSALM 68:3

OPENING PRAYER

OUR FATHER, HOW YOU DELIGHT in seeing Your sons and daughters joyful and happy before You. We can tend toward grumpiness instead, however. Remind us, we pray, of all that You have provided to ensure our happiness. In Jesus' name, amen.

INTRODUCTION

The quest for happiness fuels more activity in our society than anything else. After all, it's listed in the Declaration of Independence, written by our founding fathers in 1776, as one of our unalienable rights: "Life, liberty, and the pursuit of happiness." Yet note that those wise men didn't say happiness was guaranteed, only that we have the right to pursue it.

Everyone wants to be happy, but not everyone defines happiness in the same way. Some believe happiness can only be achieved by accumulating a great amount of wealth or an abundance of material possessions. Others may think perfect health will sustain happiness. Or they think it is up to someone else to make them happy, so they keep trying to find the person who can. Yet there are those for whom something as simple as the gentle touch of a small child, or seeing the sun peek out from behind a cloud, can spark happiness.

We need to know what happiness means to us before we go about looking for happiness, maybe even spending a lot of time and money seeking it. Only then can we build up a reservoir of that happiness within us and share it with others. We can't force people to be happy. They can only find happiness within themselves. But we can show them what happiness looks like in our own lives.

Often Christians feel God wants them to be blessed or joyful, but they stop short of thinking God also wants them to be happy. Yet the Bible assures us that happiness is a natural benefit of a life of faith. Don't worry. Be happy!

For Reflection or Discussion

- Describe what happiness looks like in your life. In other words, what makes you happy?
- Do you believe that you are responsible for your own happiness? Why or why not?
- What could you do to increase the "happiness quotient" in your life?

Scriptures and Quotes

Happy the people to whom such blessings fall!
Happy the people whose God is the LORD!
Psalm 144:15 (RSV)

A happy heart makes the face cheerful,
but heartache crushes the spirit.
Proverbs 15:13

To the man who pleases him, God gives wisdom,
knowledge and happiness.
Ecclesiastes 2:26

I know that there is nothing better for men
than to be happy and do good while they live.
Ecclesiastes 3:12

*Happy are you when people insult you and persecute you and tell all kinds
of evil lies against you because you are my followers. Be happy and glad,
for a great reward is kept for you in heaven.*
MATTHEW 5:11–12 (GNT)

*I have said this to you, that in me you may have peace. In the world you
have tribulation; but be of good cheer, I have overcome the world.*
JOHN 16:33 (RSV)

Rejoice in the Lord always. I will say it again: Rejoice!
PHILIPPIANS 4:4

*Is any one of you in trouble? He should pray.
Is anyone happy? Let him sing songs of praise.*
JAMES 5:13

*Happiness is neither within us nor without us;
it is the union of ourselves with God.*[31]
BLAISE PASCAL

*It is not how much we have, but how much we enjoy,
that makes happiness.*[32]
CHARLES HADDON SPURGEON

MEDITATION

What better way to start each day than by reciting Psalm 118:24:
This is the day the LORD has made; We will rejoice and be glad in it
(NKJV). It doesn't say, "If everything goes our way today, we will be
glad," does it? Rather the verse implies being glad, being happy, is
a choice we make each and every day. We must will ourselves to be
happy and leave the rest to God.

In the verses we read from the Sermon on the Mount, Matthew
5:11–12, the Good News Translation of the Bible substitutes happy
for blessed in the familiar encouragement from Jesus that we should
be happy because of our reward in heaven, and the two words can be
used interchangeably. Tim McConnell, pastor and author of the book
Happy Church, sees somewhat of a distinction between them.

"*Happy* and *blessed* are two different things," he writes. "One is a comment on what we are receiving from the outside: blessing. The other is a claim on the very status of our soul: happy."

He continues, "A person does feel happy when blessed, but that doesn't mean we should say 'blessed' when we mean 'happy.' God promises the internal state of our soul will be different because of his blessing. Because of what God does for us, the soul will be filled with joy and express happiness. *Blessing produces happiness.*"[33]

Happy Church goes on to assert that of all people on earth, believers in Jesus Christ should be the happiest because we are blessed with the knowledge that our life is eternal; that whatever causes of unhappiness may inflict us in this world will all fall away some day. The aches and pains, the failing eyesight, the disappointing relationships, none of these afflictions will matter in the light of eternity. We should be happy believers comprising a happy church for the glory of God.

We can be happy people blessed by God if we believe in Jesus Christ, and thus have the power of the Holy Spirit within us to guide and encourage us. If that is our state of heart and mind, we should let it show. How can we do that? By looking for the blessing in every situation. By giving a smile or a greeting to someone we pass who looks down in the dumps. By being willing to share with those who ask why we seem so happy considering our present circumstances. By living as blessed people of God who have every reason to be happy— today and forever.

For Reflection or Discussion

- Can you remember a time in your life when you made a conscious decision to be happy despite your circumstances?
- What is the source of your happiness today?
- How might we be beacons of happiness in our world today?

A Thought to Share

If you're happy and you know it, clap your hands!

Suggestion for the Week

Be attentive to times during each day when you feel happiest. What blessing sparked your happiness? Thank God for it.

Suggested Hymns

- Joyful, Joyful, We Adore You
- Peace Like a River

Prayer Requests and Closing Prayer

LESSON 26

The Battle Is the Lord's

KEY VERSE

Who is this King of glory? The LORD strong and mighty,
the LORD mighty in battle.
PSALM 24:8

OPENING PRAYER

O LORD, SOME DAYS IT SEEMS as if we are faced with one battle after the other. We may not have to take up swords or guns to fight these battles, but they are real, nevertheless. We know, Lord, that we have victory in You! Thank You for promising us that every battle we face is Yours, not ours. In Jesus' name, amen.

INTRODUCTION

A young military wife whose husband was deployed tried to dissuade her toddler son from playing with toy guns. One person in the family in battle was enough, she reasoned, so she even asked grandparents and friends not to give her son weapons of any kind. However, as she watched him play all alone in the backyard one morning, she noticed that he picked up a stick shaped like a gun, pointed it, and said, "Bang, bang!"

Hers was a losing battle and she knew it. Why? Because little boys are created to be warriors, to be protectors and providers. He was simply a warrior in training, and there was little she could do about it. It was in his nature, and it was going to be okay.

Yet it isn't just males who have battles to face, is it? Whether male or female, we all have to battle from time to time. Some battles may be because of enemies who come against us. Others are within ourselves as we struggle with a decision or must deal with depression or another health problem. All these things can make us feel like we are in the midst of a battle without enough ammunition.

Not all is hopeless however. We can be equipped for battle. Not only can we reach out to family, friends, and service providers, but we can call on the King of Glory! When the battle is the Lord's, it's won before it ever begins. Let's always prepare for battle by handing whatever we are facing over to the Lord first. His victory is our victory. Always and forever.

For Reflection or Discussion

- Have you felt like you were in a battle recently?
- If so, what "weapons" did you have with you?
- Have you ever helped someone else fight their battles?

Scriptures and Quotes

All those gathered here will know it is not by sword or spear that the LORD saves; for the battle is the LORD's, and he will give all of you into our hands.
I Samuel 17:47

With us is the LORD our God to help us and to fight our battles.
2 Chronicles 32:8

With God we will gain the victory, and he will trample down our enemies.
Psalm 60:12

The LORD will march out like a mighty man, like a warrior he will stir up his zeal; with a shout he will raise the battle cry and will triumph over his enemies.
Isaiah 42:13

We are more than conquerors through him who loved us.
ROMANS 8:37

*But thanks be to God! He gives us the victory
through our Lord Jesus Christ.*
1 CORINTHIANS 15:57

*Finally, be strong in the Lord and in his mighty power. Put on the full
armor of God so that you can take your stand against the devil's schemes.*
EPHESIANS 6:10

*Fight the good fight of the faith. Take hold of the
eternal life to which you were called.*
1 TIMOTHY 6:12

*When we pray for the Spirit's help . . . we will simply fall down at the
Lord's feet in our weakness. There we will find the victory and power that
comes from His love.*
ANDREW MURRAY

Fight the good fight of faith, and God will give you spiritual mercies.[34]
GEORGE WHITEFIELD

MEDITATION

From our days in Sunday school with the felt board characters, we've heard of David and Goliath. Of how a mere shepherd boy courageously stood up to the biggest, meanest Philistine—a man so ferocious that all the Israeli soldiers and even King Saul himself had not stepped forward to fight him. Yet here was David, who had just been sent to the front lines to take supplies to his brothers, who said to Saul, *"Let no one lose heart on account of this Philistine, your servant will go and fight him"* (1 Samuel 17:32).

What gave David so much confidence? Not what, but Who. David put his trust in God. After refusing the armor Saul offered him, he set out for battle saying, *"The LORD who delivered me from the paw of the lion and the paw of the bear will deliver me from the hand of this Philistine"* (1 Samuel 17:37). Then armed only with his trusty sling and five smooth stones from the stream which he placed in his shepherd's bag, he ran forward to meet Goliath on the battlefield. You know the end of that encounter.

What about us? When we are faced with a battle today, do we look back to remember the battles the Lord has brought us through in the past? What metaphorical lions and bears have we defeated with God's help? What disappointments has He healed, and what fears waylaid? How many times has He shown up to fight for us? He delivered us then; won't He come through for us now?

The truth is, we can face any battle as long as the Lord is on our side. Why? Because we know the victory has already been won. Through the power of the Holy Spirit, we can confidently enter any battle life presents knowing the same God who sent His Son to die for us on the cross will see us through to victory. The battle is the Lord's. Trust Him to fight it.

FOR REFLECTION OR DISCUSSION

- Can you remember a past battle that you were in?
- Did you call on the Lord for help?
- How did that work out for you?

A THOUGHT TO SHARE

We don't fight for victory—we fight from victory!

SUGGESTION FOR THE WEEK

If you feel like you are in the midst of a battle this week, don't do anything until you have turned it over to the Lord in prayer. He's got your back.

SUGGESTED HYMNS

- Lead On, O King Eternal
- Onward, Christian Soldiers
- Stand Up, Stand Up for Jesus

PRAYER REQUESTS AND CLOSING PRAYER

LESSON 27

Trust and Obey

KEY VERSE

The eternal God commanded that it be made known.
God wanted all the Gentiles to obey him by trusting in him.
ROMANS 16:26 (NIRV)

OPENING PRAYER

O GOD, HOW WE LONG TO trust in You with all our hearts and souls. Once we trust, we know Your blessings may abound if we also obey You. Teach us to trust and obey, Lord. For our benefit and Your glory. In Jesus' name we pray, amen.

INTRODUCTION

Everyone trusts in something. A passenger traveling by air climbs aboard the airplane and buckles the seat belt trusting that the plane will land safely at the destination. A competitive diver on a springboard soars up into the air trusting that there is water below to soften the landing. A beaming bride says "I do" trusting that her groom will keep his vows until they are separated by death.

In all three examples, there's an element of obedience present too. The airline passenger must obey the captain's commands to stay in his or her seat during a turbulent flight and must obey all restrictions as to what may be brought onto a plane. The diver has no choice but to obey the laws of gravity, and in a competition, must obey the guidelines set by the governing body and the judges. The bride? In a traditional wedding, she often promises to "love and obey" her husband, knowing such submission will lead to the balance and mutual love they both desire.

Perhaps there is no more apparent example of the connection between trusting and obeying, however, than in the relationship between a parent and child. From infancy, the child learns to trust the face of the mom or dad who comes in to pick him up from his crib when he cries. In time, he learns to trust that his parent will also feed him, dress him to protect him from the elements, and keep him safe in all ways. Though his rebellious nature will no doubt kick in at some point, it's easier for the child to obey his parents because he first trusted in them and found them to be trustworthy.

So it is with our relationship with God. Once we know Him, we trust Him. Once we trust Him, we find it easier to obey Him. In fact, we can't truly love Him and receive His complete love and blessing for us until we trust and obey—there's no better way.

For Reflection or Discussion

- In what events do you trust on a daily basis?
- Why do you trust the people that you trust?
- Do you find it easy or difficult to be obedient?

Scriptures and Quotes

Some trust in chariots and some in horses,
but we trust in the name of the LORD our God.
PSALM 20:7

He will have no fear of bad news; his heart is steadfast,
trusting in the LORD.
PSALM 112:7

Trust in the LORD with all your heart and lean not on
your own understanding; in all your ways acknowledge
him, and he will make your paths straight.
PROVERBS 3:5–6

You will keep in perfect peace him whose mind is steadfast,
because he trusts in you. Trust in the LORD forever,
for the LORD, the LORD, is the Rock eternal.
ISAIAH 26:3–4

He replied, "Blessed rather are those who hear
the word of God and obey it."
LUKE 11:28

Do not let your hearts be troubled. Trust in God, trust also in me.
JOHN 14:1

If anyone loves me, he will obey my teaching. My Father will love him,
and we will come to him and make our home with him.
JOHN 14:23

If you obey my commands, you will remain in my love, just as I have
obeyed my Father's commands and remain in his love.
JOHN 15:10

But if anyone obeys his word, God's love is truly made complete in him.
This is how we know we are in him: Whoever claims to live in him must
walk as Jesus did.
1 JOHN 2:5–6

Don't try to hold God's hand; let Him hold yours. Let Him do the
holding, and you do the trusting.[35]
HANMER WILLIAM WEBB-PEPLOE

MEDITATION

So why should we trust in God? The reasons are innumerable once we know who He is and all He has done for us. We can trust in Him because His word is true and He cannot lie. We can trust Him because He never changes, and He keeps all His promises. We can trust Him to be good, faithful, loving, just, forgiving, and infinitely wise not just now and again, but always.

We can also trust that God will never leave us but is on our side and wants the best for us. Above all, we can trust Him because He sacrificed His own Son so sin would no longer be a barrier between us and Him. His sacrifice means we can have eternal life with Him. In God we can trust.

With so much indisputable evidence that God can be trusted, why is it that we don't always obey the commands and directions He has given us in His holy Word, the Bible? Shouldn't obedience naturally follow trust? Why don't we always listen when He gently—or perhaps sternly—suggests to us we should take a certain path?

Our reticence to trust and obey most often comes from our human condition. We have free will, and we live in a culture that strongly suggests each of us is the master of his or her own fate. Current culture also suggests we should forge our own paths and not take direction or guidance from anyone—including God. But we might miss the very best God has planned for our lives when we give in to our sinful, self-centered human nature. Even delayed obedience can mean we miss some of the gifts and blessings God plans for us.

The good news is God doesn't give up on us. When we go off on our own, in the wrong direction, He's like the GPS system that says, "Recalculating." He will help us get back on the right path once we trust and obey at any point in our journey. Although there is no guarantee that blessings will follow when we do change our ways, so often we see them simply shower down upon us. It's never too late to trust and obey.

For Reflection or Discussion

- What do you think causes us not to trust and obey God?
- Was there a time in your life when you knew you were not following God's best plan for you?
- Have you seen any blessings result from your willingness to trust and obey God?

A Thought to Share

> *Don't just sit and rust—trust! Trust God and get moving in any direction He asks you to go.*

SUGGESTION FOR THE WEEK

Pray and ask God to show you if there is any area of your life where you are failing to trust and obey Him completely. Then do so.

SUGGESTED HYMNS

- 'Tis So Sweet to Trust in Jesus
- Trust and Obey

PRAYER REQUESTS AND CLOSING PRAYER

LESSON 28

Putting Worry to Rest

Who of you by worrying can add a single hour to his life?
LUKE 12:25

OPENING PRAYER

O LORD, WE SPEND SO MUCH time worrying about things that only You have the power to change. Help us to learn the difference between caring concern and fruitless worry, Lord. In Your name we pray, amen.

INTRODUCTION

An older couple moved into a house in a new neighborhood. When the wife heard there had once been a burglary in another house on their street, she couldn't stop worrying that the same thing would happen to them. Every night she would ask her husband to check every door and window of their home twice to make sure all was secure.

One night the husband heard a noise downstairs. Without waking his wife, he went down to investigate. Sure enough, there was a burglar in the living room trying to disconnect the TV. "Excuse me," the husband called out. "Would you mind coming upstairs with me? My wife's been expecting you for ten years."

We can laugh about that story, and in this case something bad *did* happen, but how much of our lives have we wasted worrying about what never happens or is out of our ability to control?

We worry that a teenage granddaughter may be making bad choices, but we don't really know how she is spending her time—or that jeans with holes in them are a fashion trend and not a sign of rebellion.

We worry that a persistent headache is a brain tumor, or that a recurring pain in our abdomen means we have cancer. Our worry increases dramatically if we research our symptoms on the internet. Yes, people do get dire diagnoses, but a quick trip to the doctor often confirms there was nothing to fret about at all. We spend even more time in fruitless worry if we put off going to the doctor because we are afraid of what we might hear.

Often, there might be good reason to be concerned, especially about those we love. If we hear an adult child is caught in a blinding snowstorm on the highway, the best solution is for us to pray—to give this and other situations over to the only One who can possibly do anything about them. By doing so we can replace the harmful habit of worrying with the more productive habit of putting our worry to rest.

For Reflection or Discussion

- What do you think the difference is between worry and concern?
- How can we know that we are worrying fruitlessly?
- Do you think it's possible to make ourselves physically ill by worrying?

Scriptures and Quotes

Cast your cares on the LORD and he will sustain you;
he will never let the righteous fall.
PSALM 55:22

Search me, O God, and know my heart;
test me and know my anxious thoughts.
PSALM 139:23

Therefore I tell you, do not worry about your life, what you will eat or drink; or about your body, what you will wear. Is not life more important

than food, and the body more important than clothes? Look at the birds of the air; they do not sow or reap or store away in barns, and yet your heavenly Father feeds them. Are you not much more valuable than they?
MATTHEW 6:25–26

Therefore do not worry about tomorrow, for tomorrow will worry about itself. Each day has enough trouble of its own.
MATTHEW 6:34

Do not be afraid, little flock, for your Father has been pleased to give you the kingdom.
LUKE 12:32

Do not be anxious about anything, but in everything, by prayer and petition, with thanksgiving, present your requests to God.
PHILIPPIANS 4:6

Cast all your anxiety on him because he cares for you.
1 PETER 5:7

Do not anticipate trouble or worry about what may never happen. Keep in the sunlight.[36]
BENJAMIN FRANKLIN

Fretting stems from doubt about God's ability, or willingness to use his ability, to do the right thing in our life. We don't trust him.[37]
CYNDY SHERWOOD

MEDITATION

Worry can be defined as a feeling of apprehension, dread, or uneasiness and involves negative thoughts about the future. But for the Christian, a more accurate definition is lack of trust in God. We become anxious when we fail to rely on the faithful provisions and very presence of God and begin to rely on our own ability to fix everything. When we find ourselves worrying, or even becoming a chronic worrywart, our circumstance doesn't need our constant attention but rather our relationship with God.

How do we go about shifting our focus from worry to worship? How do we increase our trust in God and force worry to fade away—or even disappear altogether? One way is to remember all the many times God has helped us in the past. We don't have to walk as believers for long before we begin to see God's hand in the circumstances of our lives. We may not recognize His involvement at the time, but looking back we often discover He was protecting us as He worked all things together for our good.

A practical approach to worry is to accept what we cannot change and immediately take those things to God. Worry serves its only purpose when our anxiety forces us to our knees in prayer. In addition to praying, we must open the Bible and strengthen ourselves—heart, mind, and soul—with God's promises to us.

At the end of Jesus' wonderful teaching about the fruitlessness of worry in Matthew 6, He reminds us that if God cares for the birds of the air and arrays the lilies of the field, He will surely care for us. He closes with, *"But seek first his kingdom and his righteousness, and all these things will be given to you as well"* (Matthew 6:33).

We will always have concerns about the things of this world that also grieve the heart of God, but we mustn't let our concern turn to worry. Instead, we must put our worry to rest by choosing to turn it over to God. Our choice and God's power. What a glorious combination.

For Reflection or Discussion

- What does it mean to shift from worry to worship? How can worshipping God change us as well as bring Him glory?
- Was there a time in your life when you knew you needed to let go of a certain worry? What was it?
- How can we cultivate the habit of putting worry to rest?

A Thought to Share

I don't know what tomorrow holds, but I know Who holds tomorrow.

Suggestion for the Week

As you climb into bed each night this week, ask the Lord to reveal any area of worry that might keep you awake and give that issue to Him in prayer. As you know, He's up all night anyway.

Suggested Hymns

- It Is Well with My Soul
- Turn Your Eyes Upon Jesus
- What a Friend We Have in Jesus

Prayer Requests and Closing Prayer

LESSON 29

The Gift of Contentment

KEY VERSE

> *But godliness with contentment is great gain.*
> *For we brought nothing into the world,*
> *and we can take nothing out of it.*
> 1 TIMOTHY 6:6–7

OPENING PRAYER

ALMIGHTY GOD, YOU GIVE US so many blessings and we have every reason to rest contentedly in Your loving arms all the days of our lives. Forgive us, Lord, when we let our selfish wants and desires take root in our hearts. Help us to receive gratefully Your gift of contentment. In Jesus' name, amen.

INTRODUCTION

How easy it is for our hearts to begin to desire something we don't really need—or that may not even be good for us. Because we live in a prosperous nation, we are deluged with advertising from marketers wanting us to think our lives will be richer, easier, healthier even, if we buy their product. And look! It's only three easy payments!

Yes, the desire to acquire has influenced all of us at one time or another. So much so that many people purchase things on credit and then find themselves swimming in credit card debt. The average American household carries debt in the thousands according to governmental tracking agencies. Programs like Dave Ramsay's Financial Peace University teach consumers to live within their means—and advise them to cut up their credit cards. Sadly, some people simply can't bring themselves to pick up the scissors, so they give up at that point and choose to stay in debt instead.

Oscar Wilde, the Irish poet and playwright known for his wit, stated there are two tragedies in life: Not getting what we want and getting what we want. Because getting what we want doesn't always benefit us, does it? Life is too full of useless desires and harmful cravings.

Jesus sees the desires of our heart. He knows when what we want is really a sign of a deeper desire. We may think we want a new outfit so we'll fit in better, but He sees that our real need is to feel accepted and loved. So He offers that kind of contentment to us free of charge.

FOR REFLECTION OR DISCUSSION

- Can you remember a time in your life when you wanted something so badly you would do anything to get it?
- How can we know if what we desire is good for us?
- Have you ever been lacking in the essentials of life? How did that feel?

SCRIPTURES AND QUOTES

If they obey and serve him, they will spend the rest of their days in prosperity and their years in contentment.
JOB 36:11

Delight yourself in the LORD and he will give you the desires of your heart.
PSALM 37:4

I am content and at peace. As a child lies quietly in its mother's arms, so my heart is quiet within me.
PSALM 131:2 (GNT)

The fear of the LORD leads to life:
Then one rests content, untouched by trouble.
PROVERBS 19:23

I know what it is to be in need, and I know what it is to have plenty.
I have learned the secret of being content in any and every situation,
whether well fed or hungry, whether living in plenty or in want.
PHILIPPIANS 4:12

But if we have food and clothing, we will be content with that.
1 TIMOTHY 6:8

Keep your lives free from the love of money and
be content with what you have, because God has said,
"Never will I leave you; never will I forsake you."
HEBREWS 13:5

Contentment comes not to those whose means are great,
but to those whose needs are few.
ANONYMOUS

I am always content with what happens; for I know that what God
chooses is better than what I choose.[38]
EPICTETUS

Whatever comes, let's be content withall:
Among God's Blessings, there is no one small.[39]
ROBERT HERRICK

MEDITATION

A desire to acquire can rob us of our contentment, but so can our tendency to look back over our lives and second-guess our decisions or fret over past relationships. The Lord doesn't dredge up past mistakes and failures and bring them to mind, however. The Evil One wants to take away any contentment we find in the Lord. But we mustn't let him succeed.

Even our biblical heroes weren't immune to second-guessing themselves, however. In Joshua 7:7 we read: *And Joshua said, "Ah, Sovereign LORD, why did you ever bring this people across the Jordan to deliver us into the hands of the Amorites to destroy us? If only we had been content to stay on the other side of the Jordan!"* Did you notice two words that often plague us in that scripture verse? They are "if only." We tend to think: If only I hadn't married him in the first place. If only I'd stayed in school. If only I'd had children someone would be around to care for me now. We can easily be plagued by the "if onlys."

We can also be tortured by the "shouldas." I should have said something more, or maybe something less, to that person who accused me falsely. I should have taken better care of my body at a younger age. I should have followed my mother's advice and gone to church. So many "shouldas" we accumulate in life!

After his early history of persecuting Christians, "if onlys" and "shouldas" could have derailed the Apostle Paul's ministry. Instead, he said, *Forgetting what is behind and straining toward what is ahead, I press on toward the goal to win the prize for which God has called me heavenward in Christ Jesus* (Philippians 3:13–14).

We can do that too. By trusting in Jesus as the true and only Source of our contentment, we can come to the end of our lives and say, like Paul, *I have learned the secret of being content in any and every situation* (Philippians 4:12). Knowing that as believers in Jesus Christ we have His gift of salvation, we have every reason to be content regardless of our circumstances. We must not let the world and its desires, the "if onlys" and the "shouldas," rob us of the gift of contentment our Lord so readily offers to us.

FOR REFLECTION OR DISCUSSION

- Is there an "if only" or a "shoulda" robbing you of your contentment today? How can you keep it from nagging at you?
- Even biblical heroes second-guessed themselves. How does developing this habit rob us of our peace and contentment?
- How easy or difficult is it for you to "press on toward the goal" as Paul said? Is there anything holding you back?

A THOUGHT TO SHARE

Be content in the moment, and you'll be content in the day.
Be content in the day, and you'll be content in life.

Suggestion for the Week

If you are plagued by "if onlys" or "shouldas" that are robbing you of your peace of mind, surrender them to God in prayer and ask Him to replace them with His gift of contentment.

Suggested Hymns

- Great Is Thy Faithfulness
- Just a Closer Walk with Thee

Prayer Requests and Closing Prayer

LESSON 30

Just Listen

KEY VERSE

My sheep listen to my voice; I know them, and they follow me.
I give them eternal life, and they shall never perish;
no one can snatch them out of my hand.
JOHN 10:27–28

OPENING PRAYER

LORD, WE HAVE SO MANY messages directed at us every day. Teach us to listen only and often to Your voice. Quiet our hearts and minds so that we can always hear You clearly. In Your precious name we pray, amen.

INTRODUCTION

A little boy was being particularly squirmy and disruptive in church during the sermon. Finally, his mother leaned over to him and said, "If you don't sit still and listen, the pastor will just have to start his sermon all over again." That did the trick.

How often are we squirmy or distracted when we should be listening? It's so easy to be thinking about something we need to do, or more commonly, something we want to say next, instead of really listening to the person who is speaking to us. Only when we focus on the other person will we walk away with a clear understanding of the message he or she intended to convey.

Many things can impact our ability to listen well. For instance, when going to a doctor's office for a consultation or to hear a complicated diagnosis, it's often important to take someone with us who can listen intently, and perhaps take notes. This is necessary because, if we hear one thing that concerns us, we may not be able to hear anything else that is said. We then might leave with misunderstandings that could not only upset us but put our health at risk.

Elementary school teachers know that developing good listening habits will help a student throughout the educational process, so they sometimes have the children sit in a circle and whisper a secret from one to the next. By the time the secret gets all the way around the circle, it's often very different from the original message. A good lesson in the importance of listening carefully.

The good news is that listening is a skill we can discipline ourselves to learn. Just as we make it a point to eat healthy food or go to bed at a regular time, we can become better listeners when we make listening carefully a priority in our lives. Those with hearing challenges may become better listeners than the rest of us because they have to focus intently on what or whom they want to hear. All of us can become better listeners if we try. After all, we don't want to miss something important—especially if it is the Lord speaking to us through one of the many ways He does.

For Reflection or Discussion

- Do you have any kind of hearing loss? If so, how have you been able to compensate for it?
- How does it make you feel when you think others aren't listening to you?
- Have you ever had a serious misunderstanding with someone because he or she didn't listen well?

Scriptures and Quotes

Whether you turn to the right or to the left, your ears will hear a voice behind you saying, "This is the way; walk in it."
ISAIAH 30:21

She had a sister called Mary, who sat at the
Lord's feet listening to what he said.
LUKE 10:39

He who belongs to God hears what God says.
JOHN 8:47

Consequently, faith comes from hearing the message, and the message is
heard through the word of Christ.
ROMANS 10:17

Everyone should be quick to listen,
slow to speak and slow to become angry.
JAMES 1:19

If anyone hears my voice and opens the door, I will come in and eat with
him, and he with me.
REVELATION 3:20

None of us will be hearing from God in a consistent, ongoing fashion
until we consciously, deliberately clear away the clutter, create the margin,
and tune our attention inward to listen for what His Spirit is saying.[40]
PRISCILLA SHIRER

To listen to someone who has no one to listen
to him is a very beautiful thing.[41]
MOTHER TERESA

MEDITATION

Jesus often took the time to listen to those around Him. He heard their pleas for personal healing and their desperate cries for others who were ill or dying. He listened and He responded.

A man who prayed often was surprised to find he would get messages from the Lord meant for those for whom he prayed. He came to call these gifts "listening prayers." When he brought someone he knew before the Lord in prayer, the Lord would often respond with words of wisdom, encouragement, and love for that person. As the man heard these messages, he wrote them down as a special gift for the person for whom he was praying.

This man's ability to listen and hear from God in this way was a gift, but we all could hear from the Lord more often if we truly took the time to be still and listen. More likely, if we make time to pray at all, it's to throw out a list of requests to the Lord followed by a quick amen before we start our day. What if we slowed down to listen after each request? Might we hear the Lord's direction or answer deep in our spirits? If we take the time to praise Him before, during, and after praying, the lines of communication will open, and we will be able to hear and receive any message He wants to impart.

Few people have heard the audible voice of God, no matter how earnestly they pray. But many have heard silent messages in their hearts and spirits that they knew could only come from the Lord. In addition, God may choose to speak to us through His Word, through conversations with other believers, through the message of a respected pastor, or even through the beauty of song or the glories of His creation. He speaks to us continuously, and in so many creative ways, if we will only listen.

FOR REFLECTION OR DISCUSSION

- What do you think keeps us from hearing from God?
- Was there a time in your life when you are sure He responded directly to you after you prayed?
- How do you hear the Lord's voice most clearly?

A THOUGHT TO SHARE

When we listen to Jesus first, we may hear
Him telling us to listen to others too.

SUGGESTION FOR THE WEEK

As you have time in prayer this week, sit in silence and listen for the Lord's response. Whether you hear an answer, know that He heard you and that your request is forever in His heart.

Suggested Hymns

- In the Garden
- Softly and Tenderly

Prayer Requests and Closing Prayer

LESSON 31

Be Courageous

KEY VERSE

Have I not commanded you? Be strong and courageous. Do not be terrified; do not be discouraged, for the LORD your God will be with you wherever you go.
JOSHUA 1:9

OPENING PRAYER

O LORD, HOW OFTEN WE LET fear keep us from doing the things You ask us to do—even from living the lives You have ordained us to live. Remind us, Lord, that we have nothing to fear because You are with us and You will embolden us. Give us courage to face this day and all the days to come. In Jesus' mighty name we pray, amen.

INTRODUCTION

Oh, how children love superheroes! In our time it may have been Mighty Mouse who saved the day, but now little ones love to dress up as Spider-Man, Batman, Wonder Woman, and so many others. The popularity of some of these superheroes and heroines has spanned several generations.

Two small brothers wore costumes to their older brother's ballgame. One wore a blue and yellow Batman suit with a small mask over his eyes, and the other wore a black suit with a full mask. "I'm old school Batman," said the smaller of the two. "I'm new school Batman!" his brother exclaimed.

What is it about supernatural power that attracts us so? Maybe it's because we know our own physical limitations all too well. The older we grow the harder it is to ignore that we can't do all the activities we enjoyed in years past. We may even struggle with the most basic mobility skills because of failing joints or weak muscles. We need a courageous hero for sure.

Even Hollywood knows our attraction to courage. Every action movie has what's known as the "armament scene." The good guys are getting their weapons ready, assembling their forces, before going out to fight the bad guys. The music builds to a fever pitch, and then we know the struggle between the forces of good and evil will soon follow. Only the heroes will emerge victorious, and we count on them to be courageous.

In reality, there is only one who can truly save us, however, and that is Jesus Christ. Once we have Him in our hearts, we can be courageous as we trust that the battle is His. He will give us all the power we need to face each day, and every circumstance, courageously.

For Reflection or Discussion

- Who was your favorite superhero when you were growing up?
- Can you recall helping your children dress up as superheroes?
- If you had a superhero in your life today, what would you ask him to do for you?

Scriptures and Quotes

See, the Sovereign LORD comes with power, and his arm rules for him.
ISAIAH 40:10

But Jesus immediately said to them:
"Take courage! It is I. Don't be afraid."
MATTHEW 14:27

Be on your guard; stand firm in the faith; be courageous; be strong.
1 CORINTHIANS 16:13 (NIV, 2011)

Finally, be strong in the Lord and in his mighty power.
EPHESIANS 6:10

*I eagerly expect and hope that I will in no way be ashamed, but will have
sufficient courage so that now as always Christ will be exalted in my body,
whether by life or by death. For to me, to live is Christ and to die is gain.*
PHILIPPIANS 1:20–21

*For God did not give us a spirit of timidity,
but a spirit of power, of love and of self-discipline.*
2 TIMOTHY 1:7

*But Christ is faithful as a son over God's house.
And we are his house, if we hold on to
our courage and the hope of which we boast.*
HEBREWS 3:6

*Do not be afraid. I am the First and the Last. I am the Living One;
I was dead, and behold I am alive for ever and ever!*
REVELATION 1:17–18

Faith is having the courage to let God have control.
ANONYMOUS

MEDITATION

What is courage, really? Is it rushing into a burning building to
save lives, or being willing to get up and get dressed each day when
you feel like staying in bed? Is it running for public office, or taking
time to tell someone gently why you believe in the Lord as you do?

In truth, courage wears many faces. It's the tear-stained face of
the pregnant young woman determined to carry her baby to term
although tests reveal potential birth defects. It's the resolute face of
the soldier hugging his family goodbye as he leaves for yet another
deployment. It's the weary face of a single mom working two jobs to
put food on the table for her family.

God calls us to be courageous, but He doesn't expect for the
courage to come only from our own reserves. Rather He promises He
will be with us when a situation arises that requires more courage,

more strength, than we can muster alone. We must keep our eyes on Him, however.

The disciple Peter learned this lesson the hard way. In Matthew 14, we read the account of the time the disciples went ahead of Jesus in a boat while he stayed behind to pray. As the wind buffeted the waves all around them, they noticed a figure coming toward them, walking on the water proclaiming, *"Take courage! It is I. Don't be afraid"* (Matthew 14:27).

"Lord, if it's you," Peter replied, *"tell me to come to you on the water"* (Matthew 14:28). Jesus told him to come, so he got out of the boat and was walking toward Jesus on the water. He became frightened when he saw the wind and the waves. He took his eyes off Jesus, and that's when he began to sink. Jesus reached down to save him and help him into the boat.

What is it that causes you to take your eyes off Jesus? Is it fear? Discouragement? Pain? Whatever it is, have the courage to keep your eyes on Him, and He will bring you through your storm.

For Reflection or Discussion

- Do you think of yourself as a courageous person? Why or why not?
- Was there a time in your life when you relied on God to give you the courage you needed in a certain situation?
- How can we grow in courage as we age?

A Thought to Share

Courage is fear that has said its prayers.

Suggestion for the Week

Where does your courage fail you? Take those situations to God and ask Him to give you all the courage you need to live a victorious life in Him.

Suggested Hymns

- Stand Up, Stand Up for Jesus
- Turn Your Eyes upon Jesus

Prayer Requests and Closing Prayer

LESSON 32

Eternity Now

KEY VERSE

Now this is eternal life: that they may know you, the only true God, and Jesus Christ, whom you have sent.
JOHN 17:3

OPENING PRAYER

LORD, THOSE WHO BELIEVE IN Your Son know we are promised eternal life once we die. But Lord, you say we have it the moment we trust in You. Help us to live like people who know our eternal future *and* our eternal present. In Jesus' name, amen.

INTRODUCTION

"Nothing lasts forever," we are told. Or maybe you remember hearing, "All good things must come to an end." It's possible someone has even told you, "Enjoy your health while it lasts. People weren't made to live forever." All these adages have some truth to them when we look at them with earthly eyes, but kingdom eyes see a different truth.

People are fascinated with trying to extend the natural life expectancy, and modern science has had some success with that. There are more people over a hundred, otherwise known as centenarians, than ever before in our country's history. Often at a celebratory gathering they are asked for the secret to their amazing longevity. Answers vary from "have a glass of wine every day," or "marry well," to "think about other people more than yourself." Inheriting good genes helps, but clearly there's no one formula for living a long life.

In truth, we aren't like the latest appliances and vehicles with their extended warranties. Buyers pay for these because they know nothing is made to last like it used to. We can't even say our existence here on earth is as guaranteed as one of those long-life light bulbs we may have purchased from a door-to-door salesman in the past. In fact, the light from those bulbs may well continue to burn on earth longer than our own lights do.

No, there are no guarantees on our health, and our days are numbered. Yet what we can know for sure is that as believers in Jesus Christ, we don't have an expiration date. We have a guarantee that is rock solid. We have eternal life, and we have it right here and now.

For Reflection or Discussion

- Have you ever purchased something that broke before you thought it should?
- If you could ask your doctor for an extended warranty on your health, would you sign up for it?
- What would you say if someone asked you for the secret to a long and healthy life?

Scriptures and Quotes

You have made known to me the path of life; you will fill me with joy in your presence, with eternal pleasures at your right hand.
PSALM 16:11

How great are his signs, how mighty his wonders! His kingdom is an eternal kingdom; his dominion endures from generation to generation.
DANIEL 4:3

For God so loved the world that he gave his one and only Son, that whoever believes in him shall not perish but have eternal life.
JOHN 3:16

*I tell you the truth, whoever hears my word and believes
him who sent me has eternal life and will not be condemned;
he has crossed over from death to life.*
JOHN 5:24

*My sheep listen to my voice; I know them, and they follow me.
I give them eternal life, and they shall never perish;
no one can snatch them out of my hand.*
JOHN 10: 27–28

*For the wages of sin is death, but the gift of God is eternal life in Christ
Jesus our Lord.*
ROMANS 6:23

*For our light and momentary troubles are achieving for us an eternal
glory that far outweighs them all.*
2 CORINTHIANS 4:17

*Fight the good fight of the faith. Take hold of the eternal
life to which you were called when you made your good
confession in the presence of many witnesses.*
1 TIMOTHY 6:12

*Praise Him for his gift of eternal life and for his desire to bestow eternal,
not just temporal, gifts upon you.*[42]
CYNTHIA HEALD

MEDITATION

People all over the world bought tickets in advance and still stood in line for hours to see the exhibit of King Tut artifacts traveling from museum to museum. Known as the "Gold Pharaoh," King Tutankhamun's reign was short and unremarkable, yet no other Egyptian king was entombed with so many precious treasures.

Those touring the exhibit gaze upon amazing pieces of gold jewelry, gold swords, and more. The exhibit even includes a gold "wishing cup" engraved with King Tut's name and his wish for eternal life. His remains still reside in Luxor (formerly Thebes), Egypt, and were discovered along with his riches in 1922 nested in three coffins, the innermost one being of pure gold and the other two of wood gilded with gold. So much gold. Yet he died of malaria at the young age of nineteen and left no heirs.

Over a thousand years after King Tut's reign, Jesus was approached by a young ruler who said, *"Good teacher, what must I do to inherit eternal life?"* (Luke 18:18). Perhaps Jesus saw in this man's eyes a lust for gold not unlike that of the Egyptian kings. So, Jesus told him, *"Sell everything you have and give to the poor, and you will have treasure in heaven. Then come, follow me"* (Luke 18:22).

Scripture reveals that this wealthy man became sad and walked away. The price Jesus asked of him was too great. We can only wonder which of his treasures came to mind as he made his decision. Was it his new chariot? His house on the hill? The jewel-encrusted necklace he just gave his wife? Whatever it was that held him back, it was worthless compared to the gift of eternal life.

What about us? Do we ever hold on to worthless things instead of surrendering all to Jesus and accepting eternal life in return? Remember, even if we're buried with our material possessions, we can't really take them with us. But maybe we grasp something besides our earthly treasures. Some may hold on to their pride, refusing to believe they need a Savior at all. Others hold on to their guilt and shame, mistakenly thinking their sins can never be forgiven. Today is not too late to surrender all to Jesus and accept His gift of eternal life. Let's begin living our eternal lives today.

For Reflection or Discussion

- Have you ever seen the King Tut exhibit or one like it? How did it make you feel?
- Is there any area of your life that you have not laid at the foot of the cross?
- How might it change your perspective to think of yourself as already living an eternal life?

A Thought to Share

Don't grow too attached to the here and now.
Our present time is only the beginning of eternity.

Suggestion for the Week

If you face a difficult situation this week, approach the problem with the perspective of a person living an eternal life.

Suggested Hymns

- Immortal, Invisible
- I Surrender All
- Lead On, O King Eternal

Prayer Requests and Closing Prayer

Lesson 33

Living Water

Key Verse

Jesus answered, "Everyone who drinks this water will be thirsty again, but whoever drinks the water I give him will never thirst. Indeed, the water I give him will become in him a spring of water welling up to eternal life."
John 4:13–14

Opening Prayer

O Lord, how thirsty we can become. Thirsty for truth, for justice, for mercy, and for the living water You offer that leads to eternal life. Thank You, Lord, for blessing us with living water to sustain us now and forever. In Your name we pray, amen.

Introduction

A woman purchased three pots of geraniums for her back patio. She faithfully watered and fed all three plants equally, yet one seemed to flourish much more than the other two. The magnificent one had between fifteen and twenty blossoms at one time while the others only managed to produce three or four. She couldn't understand why one was doing so much better until her husband told her, "The geranium on the left also gets watered by our sprinkler system." The extra water made the difference.

Water is life giving and life sustaining. When we don't have enough of it, we are desperate for it. Just enough water is a glorious gift to all living things, while too much can bring devastation in the form of flooding and other disasters.

After a period of drought in the West, the rain was welcome the day it finally came. Residents remember that it began as a misty feeling in the air. Soon the first distinct drops began to fall. All day long the ground was bathed in gentle, soaking rain. After months of no precipitation at all, the very sound of it soothed people's souls as it danced on the rooftops, collected in the gutters, and trickled down the windowpanes. By afternoon, when it was still raining, they could almost begin to see the grass turn greener. Kids on their way home from school splashed and laughed their way through puddles and birds frolicked wherever pools collected. Glorious, life-giving rain.

As critical as water is for sustaining life on earth, however, there is another kind of water that is even more important to us. Jesus said He came to bring living water, *"a spring of water welling up to eternal life"* (John 4:14). Only when we receive the water which He gives will our thirst be completely satisfied.

For Reflection or Discussion

- Have you ever experienced a severe drought? What was it like and how did you survive?
- How does a rainy day make you feel?
- Do you think we tend to take for granted having just enough water?

Scriptures and Quotes

Then will the lame leap like a deer, and the mute tongue shout for joy. Water will gush forth in the wilderness and streams in the desert.
Isaiah 35:6

My people have committed two sins: They have forsaken me, the spring of living water, and have dug their own cisterns, broken cisterns that cannot hold water.
Jeremiah 2:13

O LORD, the hope of Israel, all who forsake you will be put to shame. Those who turn away from you will be written in the dust because they have forsaken the LORD, the spring of living water.
JEREMIAH 17:13

Jesus answered her, "If you knew the gift of God and who it is that asks you for a drink, you would have asked him and he would have given you living water."
JOHN 4:10

"Whoever believes in me, as the Scripture has said, streams of living water will flow from within him." By this he meant the Spirit, whom those who believed in him were later to receive.
JOHN 7:38–39

Never again will they hunger; never again will they thirst. The sun will not beat upon them, nor any scorching heat. For the Lamb at the center of the throne will be their shepherd; he will lead them to springs of living water. And God will wipe away every tear from their eyes.
REVELATION 7:16–17

The Spirit and the bride say, "Come!" And let him who hears say, "Come!" Whoever is thirsty, let him come; and whoever wishes, let him take the free gift of the water of life.
REVELATION 22:17

Those who trust in Christ never need to look outside themselves for satisfaction because He dwells within them, supplying every emotional and spiritual need. They will never be without water again.[43]
CHARLES R. SWINDOLL

MEDITATION

It's staggering to learn how many people in the world don't have easy access to clean, safe water in their homes for drinking, cooking, washing, or bathing. Indeed, it's safe to say millions of people around the world face that challenge every day. The task for providing the water for households falls primarily on women and girls. It's estimated that the average time spent walking to collect safe water is thirty minutes, yet many must walk for hours every day just to find it.

Women were the primary water gatherers in Jesus' day, too. The water jug is often a symbol of this life-giving role women played and still play today. So, it was not surprising for Jesus to come across a Samaritan woman drawing water from a well, the account we read in John 4. Her timing was unusual. She came in the middle of the day instead of in the morning when most of the village women drew their water. We learn a bit about her reputation. She had five husbands and was now with a man not her husband, so that may explain why she avoided the others.

Jesus knew He would find her there—in fact He traveled out of his way just to see her. To her utter shock He asked her for a drink of water, a surprise because He, a man, spoke to her, a woman and a Samaritan.

We don't know if she gave Him a drink, but scripture reveals He turned His focus on her thirst, not His own. *"If you knew the gift of God and who it is that asks you for a drink, you would have asked him and he would have given you living water"* (John 4:10), He said. The discussion continues and results in Jesus revealing Himself to her as the Messiah. Then she runs back to the village and cries out to the people, *"Come, see a man who told me everything I ever did. Could this be the Christ?"* (v. 29).

How far would you go to gather water if you had none? More important, how far would you go to gather the living water leading to eternal life that Jesus promises? Would you go all the way to your knees? All the way to the cross? Certainly, neither would be too far to go to receive His gift of salvation.

For Reflection or Discussion

- What do you think Jesus means by living water?
- Do you have an unending source of living water in you?
- Have you ever shared the gospel with someone and so given them a drink of living water?

A Thought to Share

When you thirst, be sure you draw water from the right well.

Suggestion for the Week

Should someone ask you for a drink this week, ask them if they'd like some living water instead. Then tell them about Jesus.

Suggested Hymns

- Come, Thou Fount of Every Blessing
- Nothing but the Blood of Jesus

Prayer Requests and Closing Prayer

LESSON 34

The Good Shepherd

KEY VERSE

I am the good shepherd. The good shepherd lays down his life for the sheep.
JOHN 10:11

OPENING PRAYER

O LORD, HOW OFTEN WE, LIKE sheep, have gone astray. In those times, how faithfully and gently You lead us back to safety in Your loving arms. Please continue to protect us and guide us, we pray. In Jesus' name, amen.

INTRODUCTION

Author and speaker Sheila Walsh once included in her presentation a story about the bummer lambs she saw when growing up in Scotland. Bummer lambs are those who are rejected by their mothers after birth. It's possible a bummer lamb is rejected because it is one of twins and the mother doesn't have enough milk for it. Or, as Sheila said, maybe the ewe is simply older and "frankly quite tired of the whole business."

Regardless of the reason for their rejection, bummer lambs won't make it unless the shepherd intervenes. So, he takes the little lamb home, wraps it in warm blankets, holds it close to him, and feeds it from a bottle until it is strong and hearty enough to join the flock.

Sheila said that, as a child, she loved to hear the shepherds calling, "Sheep, sheep, sheep" to their flocks every morning and watching those who had been bummer lambs run to him first. They responded so quickly because they knew the shepherd's voice. It's not that they were loved more than the others—it's just that they knew they were loved.

But shepherds do much more than nurse bummer lambs. The work of the shepherd isn't as peaceful and pastoral as often portrayed. Shepherds must stand watch against predators at all times and chase after sheep that go astray. They might be exposed to the elements and the dangers themselves. Theirs is a sacrificial job.

Jesus says He is our Good Shepherd. Often the believer who has experienced pain and rejection in life, the bummer lamb if you will, comes most readily when Jesus calls and is most grateful for His care and protection. All of us should respond gratefully to Jesus, for He is the best Shepherd of all—the Shepherd of our souls.

For Reflection or Discussion

- Have you had any experience caring for sheep?
- Why is it that the bummer lambs recognize the shepherd's voice first?
- Have you ever been a shepherd of people—even small children?

Scriptures and Quotes

The LORD is my Shepherd, I shall not be in want. He makes me lie down in green pastures, he leads me beside quiet waters, he restores my soul.
PSALM 23:1–3

He tends his flock like a shepherd: He gathers the lambs in his arms and carries them close to his heart; he gently leads those who have young.
ISAIAH 40:11

The Lord their God will save them on that day as the flock of his people. They will sparkle in his land like jewels in a crown.
ZECHARIAH 9:16

If a man owns a hundred sheep, and one of them wanders away, will he not leave the ninety-nine on the hills and go to look for the one that wandered off? And if he finds it, I tell you the truth, he is happier about that one sheep than about the ninety-nine that did not wander off.
MATTHEW 18:12–13

I am the good shepherd; I know my sheep and my sheep know me.
JOHN 10:14

My sheep listen to my voice; I know them, and they follow me. I give them eternal life, and they shall never perish; no one can snatch them out of my hand.
JOHN 10:27–28

And when the Chief Shepherd appears, you will receive the crown of glory that will never fade away.
1 PETER 5:4

For the Lamb at the center of the throne will be their shepherd; he will lead them to springs of living water. And God will wipe away every tear from their eyes.
REVELATION 7:17

Trust is at the heart of allowing the Lord to shepherd us. It is believing that if He withholds something we want, He has good reasons for doing so—reasons that we may never know or understand.[44]
CYNTHIA HEALD

The staggering fact remains that Christ, the Creator of such an enormous universe of overwhelming magnitude, deigns to call Himself my Shepherd and invites me to consider myself His sheep—His special object of affection and attention. Who better could care for me?[45]
W. PHILLIP KELLER

MEDITATION

Not only is Jesus, the Son of God, our Good Shepherd, but He is also the Lamb who takes away the sin of the world. In His death on the cross, Jesus made the final sacrifice for sin. He became the sacrificial lamb so no other sacrifices of atonement would be needed.

In that one act, He defeated sin *and* death as He made a way for all who believe to have eternal life. We who believe are the blessed beneficiaries.

The Jewish people were familiar with the unblemished lamb required for a proper and adequate animal sacrifice to God. Yet their sacrifices had to be made again and again, and still today most fail to recognize that Jesus came to be the final sacrifice once and for all.

What about us? Do we truly accept Jesus not only as our Good Shepherd who guides us and cares for us, but as the Lamb who was sacrificed for us? Or do we mistakenly believe that there is something we must do, some additional sacrifice we must make, to be in good stead with God and assured of eternal life? In other words, will we follow Jesus as our Shepherd, and will we accept His sacrifice as enough?

Throughout the New Testament we read accounts of people who quickly knew that Jesus was someone worthy of following. As He called each of His twelve disciples, they didn't hesitate about leaving their homes, families, and careers to follow Jesus. Those who were fishermen literally let go of their nets and followed Him.

His call to "follow me" is as compelling today as it was then. Are people today as eager to respond as the disciples were, or do we grasp too tightly to the lives we have created for ourselves? Jesus is the Good Shepherd and all He sacrificed for us was enough. Even if you think of yourself as a bummer lamb, He is asking you to follow Him, and the only sensible response is, "Yes, Lord. Just as I am, I come."

For Reflection or Discussion

- How do we establish trust in those we follow?
- What does it mean to you that Jesus is your Good Shepherd?
- Have you answered His call to follow Him? If not, would you consider doing so today?

A Thought to Share

You don't need to know where you're going
if you're following the right Shepherd.

Suggestion for the Week

If you know someone who feels as rejected as a bummer lamb, remind that person that Jesus is the Good Shepherd, the One who cares and restores.

Suggested Hymns

- He Leadeth Me
- Just As I Am
- The Lord's My Shepherd, I'll Not Want

Prayer Requests and Closing Prayer

LESSON 35

We Are Not Invisible

KEY VERSE

She gave this name to the LORD who spoke to her: "You are the God who sees me," for she said, "I have now seen the One who sees me."
GENESIS 16:13

OPENING PRAYER

O LORD, THE OLDER WE GROW the more invisible we can feel. How encouraging it is to know that You always see us. That You watch over us all day, every day, and You know us far better than we know ourselves. Thank You, precious Lord, for Your all-encompassing love for us. In Your name we pray, amen.

INTRODUCTION

A common comment coming from the lips of aging adults with enough boldness to speak the truth is, "I feel invisible." In her book *Voices of Aging*, author Missy Buchanan presents perspectives on several key topics from the point of view of the adult child and the aging parent. One elder said, "Sometimes I feel obsolete. Unnecessary. Irrelevant. Like a carton of milk whose expiration date is long past."[46] Another aging parent said, "I remember sitting in my room while my children talked about me as if I weren't even there."[47]

No one should feel so invisible. Looking into the eyes of older friends and truly listening to what they say, we can see both who they were and who they still are.

"Don't judge my story by the chapter you walked in on," reads a poignant anonymous quote. But isn't that what we do? If we meet people for the first time at the end of their lives, don't we too often forget that this is simply one chapter? Would we want those who meet us later in life to make that same error in judgment?

Whenever we meet an older person, we need to pray we'll be able to see who they were at a younger age and who they authentically are today. We should want to know about the earlier chapters of their no doubt fascinating lives and appreciate the totality of the lives they have lived. We don't want them to say, like another older person in Buchanan's book, "My life is a library filled with books that no one reads anymore—books of adventure and romance, advice and how-tos."[48] We want people to read all the chapters of our lives, and we should try to do the same for them.

From the youngest to the oldest, we can all feel invisible at times. Yet we are never invisible in God's eyes. He always sees us as we are and wherever we are, and only He sees who we will ultimately be when all the trappings of this earth fall away. Invisible? Not on His watch.

For Reflection or Discussion

- Have you ever felt invisible? Can you recall a specific time or incident?
- How can you truly see the older friends you make?
- What chapters of your own life would you want people to "read"?

Scriptures and Quotes

O Lord, you have searched me and you know me. You know when I sit and when I rise; you perceive my thoughts from afar. You discern my going out and my lying down; you are familiar with all my ways.
Psalm 139:1–3

All the days ordained for me were written in your book before one of them came to be.
Psalm 139:16

Yet to all who received him, to those who believed in his name, he gave the right to become children of God.
JOHN 1:12

But God demonstrates his own love for us in this: While we were still sinners, Christ died for us.
ROMANS 5:8

The Spirit himself testifies with our spirit that we are God's children. Now if we are children, then we are heirs—heirs of God and co-heirs with Christ.
ROMANS 8:16–17

We are therefore Christ's ambassadors, as though God were making his appeal through us.
2 CORINTHIANS 5:20

For he has rescued us from the dominion of darkness and brought us into the kingdom of the Son he loves, in whom we have redemption, the forgiveness of sins.
COLOSSIANS 1:13-14

How great is the love the Father has lavished on us, that we should be called children of God! And that is what we are!
1 JOHN 3:1

I am not what I ought to be! . . . I am not what I wish to be! . . . I am not what I hope to be. . . . I am not what I once was, . . . and acknowledge, "By the grace of God I am what I am."[49]
JOHN NEWTON

The benefits and blessings bestowed upon us as redeemed children of God are more numerous than we can count.[50]
PRISCILLA SHIRER

MEDITATION

It's impossible to feel invisible once we know who we are in God's eyes. When our identity is in Him, not in how the world sees us, we can be assured that we are seen by Him. As we read in scripture, those who believe are children of God, Christ's ambassadors in the world, heirs of the kingdom and co-heirs with Christ.

Not only are we seen, but we are rescued, forgiven, known, and loved more deeply than we can ever imagine. We are not invisible.

We began this lesson with a verse from Genesis 16 in which Hagar says, *"You are the God who sees me"* (Genesis 16:13). You may remember the story of Hagar. When Abram's wife Sarai was unable to conceive, she suggested that Abram sleep with her Egyptian maidservant, Hagar. *"Perhaps I can build a family through her,"* Sarai said (Genesis 16:2). But when Hagar became pregnant, the Bible tells us she began to despise Sarai; Sarai mistreated her, and Hagar fled into the desert. That's where God finds her and tells her what is to happen. That she is to go back and will bear a son she is to call Ishmael.

There's more to Hagar's experience, but what we need to glean from it is if God sees a rejected, pregnant maidservant hiding in the desert, He also sees us. He sees us as we rise in the morning, as we lay our heads down at night, and all the minutes and hours in between. He sees us, He knows us, and He loves us lavishly. We are not invisible to Him.

How should knowing who we are in God's eyes change us? At a minimum, it should make us walk a little taller or hold our heads a bit higher. It should give us the confidence to share what God has done for us with others so they can also be children of God. It should give us hope that just as He sees us now, He will fulfill His promise to take us into His presence one day. Then we will see Him face-to-face and know without a doubt He also sees us.

FOR REFLECTION OR DISCUSSION

- Have you ever felt as desolate and dejected as Hagar?
- Do you also have a story of being found by God?
- What difference does it make to you knowing that God sees you?

A THOUGHT TO SHARE

Whenever you feel invisible, remember who you are in God's eyes.

Suggestion for the Week

Take time to visit with someone you don't know well. Ask about all the chapters of his or her life so that person will truly feel visible to you.

Suggested Hymns

- I Am a Child of God
- In the Garden
- Open My Eyes, That I May See

Prayer Requests and Closing Prayer

LESSON 36

The Peace of Heaven

KEY VERSE

For God was pleased to have all his fullness dwell in him, and through him to reconcile to himself all things, whether things on earth or things in heaven, by making peace through his blood, shed on the cross.
COLOSSIANS 1:19–20

OPENING PRAYER

LORD, THERE ARE TIMES HERE on earth when we long for the peace of heaven. We can't begin to know all we will experience in Your presence, but we know all things will be reconciled and we will have peace. Stay close to us, Lord, and bring us home to You in Your time. In Jesus' name, amen.

INTRODUCTION

We take a bite of lemon meringue pie and sigh, "Ooooo, that's heavenly." Or someone might mention a heavenly beach vacation spot or say the choir sounded heavenly on a particular Sunday. But how do we know what heaven is like? Can we even imagine what our senses will experience when we are finally in heaven? Not really.

Truth often comes "out of the mouths of babes," but even small children have a hard time describing heaven when asked to do so. They say things like:

"It's where God listens to prayers."

"It's a peaceful place where no one hurts."

"There are cloud houses and we can jump on the clouds."

"There are no bad guys or wars in heaven."
"We'll have bread there but not cereal."
"It's where people play games—like puzzles."
"A place where I can ride on a lion."
"It will have all the colors of glitter, but mostly pink and purple."

We smile at these innocent attempts to describe heaven, but do adults manage to do any better? All the descriptions the little children come up with are just as valid as our own perceptions of heaven, if not more so.

Maybe we can't describe heaven, but we can be sure heaven will be peaceful. We are assured of this by our key verse and by many other scripture verses describing the reconciliation that is present in heaven because Jesus Christ, the Prince of Peace, reigns there, and His peace is perfect. He provided a way for sinners to be forgiven and dwell in the presence of God. He made heaven an indescribable but desirable destination for all who believe.

For Reflection or Discussion

- Has your perception of heaven changed over the years? How?
- Do you believe heaven is an actual place?
- What would you want children to know about heaven?

Scriptures and Quotes

Whom have I in heaven but you?
And earth has nothing I desire besides you.
Psalm 73:25

My help comes from the Lord, the Maker of heaven and earth.
Psalm 121:2

Give thanks to the God of heaven. His love endures forever.
Psalm 136:26

You will keep in perfect peace him whose mind is steadfast,
because he trusts in you.
Isaiah 26:3

Peace I leave with you; my peace I give you. I do not give to you as the world gives. Do not let your hearts be troubled and do not be afraid.
JOHN 14:27

Do not be anxious about anything, but in everything, by prayer and petition, with thanksgiving, present your requests to God. And the peace of God, which transcends all understanding, will guard your hearts and your minds in Christ Jesus.
PHILIPPIANS 4:6–7

Now may the Lord of peace himself give you peace at all times and in every way. The Lord be with all of you.
2 THESSALONIANS 3:16

Heaven would hardly be heaven if we could define it.
WILLIAM E. BIEDERWOLF

Where there is peace, God is.[51]
GEORGE HERBERT

MEDITATION

The Bible gives us a physical description of heaven through the vision the Apostle John received when he was in exile in Patmos, as recorded in the Book of Revelation. John describes the river of life, the tree of life, and a great street running through the city. He even writes of a New Jerusalem where *the wall was made of jasper, and the city of pure gold, as pure as glass. The foundations of the city walls were decorated with every kind of precious stone* (Revelation 21:18–19).

Yet even with John's vision, many of our questions about heaven remain unanswered. Will we really have mansions to live in as Jesus promised in John 14:2 (KJV)—places He prepared for us in advance? Will we recognize those who already passed from this life to the next, and will they recognize us? Will there be work to do in heaven? Will we be able to observe what is happening on earth? So many questions.

We can't know everything about heaven, but once we study all the verses about it in God's Holy Word, we can have *the peace of God, which transcends all understanding* (Philippians 4:7). We have peace in knowing that, in heaven, we will be in the presence of God. We can rest assured heaven will be a wonderful place—a place where tears are wiped away. We find peace in knowing heaven is a place where all our needs are met and all our pains are gone and where God's love and mercy encompass us. That's heavenly peace, and it is guaranteed to all who believe in Jesus as their Lord and Savior.

But what about now? Can we have the peace of heaven as we go through our daily lives here on earth? It is possible. Knowing that perfect peace will be ours in heaven gives us hope and can make any situation we face here on earth easier to bear. Others may think, "How can he or she seem so peaceful in light of this situation or that diagnosis?" But it's possible for us not only to appear peaceful but to feel peaceful when we have the peace of Jesus deep in our hearts. Because of Him we carry the peace of heaven with us always.

For Reflection or Discussion

- What questions do you still have about heaven?
- Have you felt the peace of heaven in the midst of trouble?
- How can we bring the peace of heaven to others?

A Thought to Share

When you need some heavenly peace, search your redeemed heart first.

Suggestion for the Week

If you come across someone who seems particularly distraught this week, pray with them and for them. Ask the Lord to give them the peace of heaven.

Suggested Hymns

- It Is Well with My Soul
- Peace Like a River
- Peace, Perfect Peace

Prayer Requests and Closing Prayer

All God's Creatures

KEY VERSE

> *Let everything that has breath praise the LORD.*
> PSALM 150:6

OPENING PRAYER

LORD, OF ALL THE THINGS You give us to bring us joy, surely Your sweet creatures are near the top of the list. We love our pets, Lord, and we marvel at the wildlife we get to glimpse now and then. We see Your creative hand in each precious life. Thank you, Lord, for earthly creatures. In Jesus' name we pray, amen.

INTRODUCTION

America is certainly a country that loves its pets. One survey of pet owners determined that 94.2 million cats reside in US households, as do 89.7 million dogs. While there are more dog households than cat households, evidently cat owners are more likely to believe two or more are better than one. And even those numbers may not include the cats and dogs who live in shops or assisted living residences.

In addition to cats and dogs, the survey showed birds, fish, small animals, and reptiles are also kept as pets. US pet industry expenditures for things like vet visits and treatments, food, toys, beds, grooming, and vitamins equal over 75 billion dollars each year.

Hearing those totals, it's easy to despair over the amount of money spent on animals. Some may ask whether it couldn't be better used to feed starving children in developing countries or to solve the world's homeless population problem. There's an argument to be made for those better causes, but it's not likely that people will give up their fondness for animals anytime soon. In the search for unconditional love and acceptance, it's hard to beat having a golden retriever greet you at the door at the end of a long day or having a soft cat curl up in your lap and purr while you are watching TV. We love our pets and they love us so well in return.

Even if owning a pet doesn't make economic sense, might it make some emotional or spiritual sense? It's been proven that pets can calm anxiety in their owners and decrease feelings of loneliness. We know that every single animal was created by God, so being with animals brings us closer to Him also.

The puppies lined up to nurse their mother and the elk bugling in the mountain air are all really His. We take great delight in marveling at God's creation wherever we find it, and we give Him thanks for all the amazing creatures He has given us. Or has He just loaned them to us?

For Reflection or Discussion

- Can you recall a favorite pet from your childhood?
- Do you have a pet now? What was the last pet you had?
- If you chose to have pets in your homes over the years, why did you?

Scriptures and Quotes

God made the wild animals according to their kinds, the livestock according to their kinds, and all the creatures that move along the ground according to their kinds. And God saw that it was good.
Genesis 1:25

Then God said, "Let us make man in our image, in our likeness, and let them rule over the fish of the sea and the birds of the air, over the livestock, over all the earth, and over all the creatures that move along the ground."
Genesis 1:26

You are to bring into the ark two of all living creatures, male and female,
to keep them alive with you.
GENESIS 6:19

How many are your works, O LORD! In wisdom you made them all; the
earth is full of your creatures.
PSALM 104:24

The wolf will live with the lamb, the leopard will lie
down with the goat, the calf and the lion and the
yearling together; and a little child will lead them.
ISAIAH 11:6

See, your king comes to you, gentle and riding on a donkey.
MATTHEW 21:5

All things bright and beautiful,
All creatures great and small,
All things wise and wonderful,
The Lord God made them all.[52]
CECIL FRANCES ALEXANDER

If you have men who will exclude any of God's creatures
from the shelter of compassion and pity, you will have men
who will deal likewise with their fellow men.
ST. FRANCIS OF ASSISI

MEDITATION

Born into a wealthy family in 1181 in Assisi, Italy, St. Francis
spent his youth partying and carousing. After a series of visions from
God, however, he converted to a Christian life of poverty and service
and never looked back.

Known as the Patron Saint of Animals, St. Francis valued animals
so highly he preached sermons to them, according to legend. Legend
also reveals he once prayed over a wolf, convincing him to stop
attacking people and other animals. He told the wolf the villagers
would feed him if he changed his behavior, so he did.

St. Francis attracted birds wherever he went, legend says.
Reportedly he told them they should be thankful for their lives, and

they only flew away when he told them to. People reported that a flock of larks swooped near and sang at the moment of his death in 1226, honoring the one who cared for them.

Still today, many churches observe a "Blessing of the Animals" in honor of St. Francis. Children and adults bring their dogs, cats, bunnies, and other pets to church to receive a blessing. (The people may enjoy this experience more than the animals, however.)

All this is fine in moderation, yet we must be careful not to idolize our pets or other animals. Yes, we love them. Yes, we are to be good stewards of all creation, but we must remember that only man was created in God's image. As we read in Genesis 1:26, God asks us to rule over all the other creatures He created. We are to do so with compassion and love as St. Francis suggested. We donate to humane societies and advocate for the shutdown of puppy farms. We remind folks not to leave dogs in hot cars or outside in freezing temperatures, and we even have laws related to the humane treatment of pets and livestock.

We appreciate the wonderful pet therapy animals who bring smiles to the elderly or the ailing, the military or rescue dogs who save lives, and all the wildlife we are blessed to encounter. God created all the creatures, and He is no doubt pleased we enjoy them so much. May His creatures be a constant reminder of both His creative power and His unconditional love for us.

For Reflection or Discussion

- Many passages in the Bible mention animals. What animals do you remember reading about?
- How does St. Francis of Assisi's life of simple service speak to you?
- Have you ever supported an organization or cause dedicated to the welfare of animals?

A Thought to Share

If only we could be the people our pets think we are.

SUGGESTION FOR THE WEEK

This week ask someone, "If you could be any animal on earth, what would you be?" The answers will be varied and may open the door to a conversation about the extent of God's creation.

SUGGESTED HYMNS

- All Creatures of Our God and King
- This Is My Father's World

PRAYER REQUESTS AND CLOSING PRAYER

LESSON 38

Praise Him!

KEY VERSE

Praise the LORD, O my soul. I will praise the LORD all my life; I will sing praise to my God as long as I live.
PSALM 146:1–2

OPENING PRAYER

O LORD, YOU AND YOU ALONE are worthy of our praise. We lift our hearts and hands to You in praise now and forevermore. In Jesus' name, amen.

INTRODUCTION

Every year from late August to early February is football season in America. Whenever a college or NFL team plays, stadiums fill with up to 100,000 people or more to cheer their teams. Their enthusiasm is palpable. It's nearly impossible to be in one of those crowds and not get caught up in the excitement.

Why? Why do so many people spend so much money to buy tickets to games as well as hats, jerseys, or other fan gear to support their teams? Why do some go so far to show their loyalty as to travel across the country, maybe even paint their faces in team colors?

Maybe it's because being a sports fan is a fun escape from everyday life. It transports us to a competition we aren't really in but can vicariously experience—whether it ends in victory or defeat. We admire the extreme athleticism and dedication of the players on the team and the coaches. But there should be a limit to our allegiance. We need to remember that football is just a game and save all our true praise and worship not for our team, but for our God.

Where else might we be led to misplace our praise and worship? Celebrities also have fan bases and are adored and put on pedestals, often to the detriment of their own mental health and well-being. Award shows glorify performances by actors and actresses, but aren't they just doing the jobs they are paid to do the same as the waitress at the corner diner? Why should they be worthy of our praise merely because their work is displayed for all to see? The work of the waitress may have far more intrinsic value.

Clearly, the lesson here is to be careful where we place our allegiance. To resist the temptation to praise and worship anything or anyone more than our God. How much more rewarding it is for us when we praise Him. And how much delight He finds in our praise.

FOR REFLECTION OR DISCUSSION

- Have you ever been a huge fan of a sports team? Which one? Did you ever feel disappointed in your team?
- Why do you think we are tempted to identify as a fan of a certain team or celebrity?
- Was there a time in your life when you realized you allowed some other allegiance to take the place of your loyalty to God?

SCRIPTURES AND QUOTES

For great is the LORD and most worthy of praise;
he is to be feared above all gods.
1 CHRONICLES 16:25

I will praise the LORD, who counsels me;
even at night my heart instructs me.
PSALM 16:7

Why are you downcast, O my soul? Why so disturbed within me? Put your
hope in God, for I will yet praise him, my Savior and my God.
PSALM 42:5

Praise be to the Lord, to God our Savior, who daily bears our burdens.
PSALM 68:19

Praise the LORD, O my soul, and forget not all his benefits.
PSALM 103:2

Praise be to the God and Father of our Lord Jesus Christ, the Father of compassion and the God of all comfort.
2 CORINTHIANS 1:3

Praise be to the God and Father of our Lord Jesus Christ, who has blessed us in the heavenly realms with every spiritual blessing in Christ.
EPHESIANS 1:3

Praise be to the God and Father of our Lord Jesus Christ! In his great mercy he has given us new birth into a living hope through the resurrection of Jesus Christ from the dead, and into an inheritance that can never perish, spoil or fade—kept in heaven for you.
1 PETER 1:3–4

Praising God not only brings God into our situation in a powerful way, it strengthens our faith, renews our spirits, keeps our eyes on Him, and delights His heart.[53]
KIRKIE MORRISSEY

Praise can increase our faith and release the transforming power of Christ in us and our situations.[54]
RUTH MYERS

MEDITATION

So often when we step into the presence of God through prayer, we do so with a list of requests in our hand. We think more about what He can do for us than what we can give Him—our devotion, our attention, and our praise.

There's truly no wrong way to pray because God hears every prayer, but guidelines on prayer often suggest that we begin with adoration. To step into God's presence and greet Him with our praise before we make our requests known—even before we confess our sins and pray for His forgiveness. Praising God first clears our hearts and minds of the clutter keeping us from communicating with Him clearly. Praise also aligns our perspective as we remember once again who He is. He is God Almighty, Creator of all, and we are not.

Praising God has other benefits for us as well. Could Satan's discouraging messages bring us down while we are praising God? I don't think so. Can we feel sorry for ourselves and sink into a deeper depression while we are praising God? Not likely. More often than not, praising God through prayer, song, or worship lifts us higher. It lifts our countenance and it lifts our hopes. There's no doubt about it, praising God is good for us.

You may have experienced the joy praising God brings to your heart, but have you ever thought about the fact that praising God brings Him joy too? He is with us always and thinks of us always. How it must gladden His heart to know that we think of Him, too, and that we bring to Him a sacrifice of praise as we make bowing before Him a priority in our lives.

No one, and nothing we can desire or imagine, deserves praise more than our God. The Book of Revelation tells us that even the angels praise Him, singing: *Worthy is the Lamb, who was slain, to receive power and wealth and wisdom and strength and honor and glory and praise!* (Revelation 5:12). Oh, that we could make every waking moment He gives us a sacrifice of praise to our living Lord. Raise your hands and praise Him!

For Reflection or Discussion

- Can you recall a time in your life when praising God lifted you out of a worrisome situation?
- Is praising God something you do regularly in your life today?
- How do you praise Him?

A Thought to Share

> *There isn't anything we encounter in life that can't be made better by praising God.*

Suggestion for the Week

Find a quiet time this week to offer up a prayer of pure praise to the Lord. If you find yourself raising your hands and lifting your face to heaven, so much the better.

Suggested Hymns

- Doxology
- Immortal, Invisible
- Praise to the Lord, the Almighty

Prayer Requests and Closing Prayer

LESSON 39

God Is Enough

KEY VERSE

He who did not spare his own Son, but gave him up for us all—how will he not also, along with him, graciously give us all things?
ROMANS 8:32

OPENING PRAYER

LORD, WHY IS IT THAT we tend to want more when you are clearly enough to meet all our needs and satisfy all our desires? Help us, Lord. Help us to rest and trust in the knowledge You truly are all we need. You, O God, are enough. In Jesus' name, amen.

INTRODUCTION

Often when watching a game show on TV, we may observe a contestant who lets greed take hold. This player could stop where they are and have a comfortable amount of winnings, yet they persist to spin the wheel one more time or try to answer one more set of questions, only to land on "bankrupt" or give the wrong answer and lose all the winnings accumulated.

But are we much different? There is something about human nature that compels us to desire more. We may be blessed with a warm and safe place to live, but we find ourselves longing for just a bit more space, a different color of paint on the walls, or even to reside in a different state or climate. We may have children or grandchildren to love, but rather than be grateful we long for them to pay more attention to us—to spend enough time with us to know who we really are—and, of course, to absorb all the wisdom we have to share. Just having them to love doesn't seem like enough.

The ability to know when we have enough is a skill that can take a lifetime to develop, especially when it comes to wealth. The wise among us know that having too much wealth can be a burden, while having too little can be an oppression. Having the exact amount that we need to sustain us each day, perhaps with a bit stashed away for a rainy day, is a blessing we must never take for granted.

We must also learn, over the course of a lifetime, that God is always enough to supply not only our material needs, but our spiritual ones as well. We may not understand why He tarries, but He's always on time. We may not know why He withholds, but it's always in our best interest. In every situation, in the middle of every storm, God is enough when we lean on Him and count on Him to fill every gap, every longing, and every need we have.

For Reflection or Discussion

- Do you find yourself longing for more than you have in any area of your life?
- Have you thought about the blessing of having "just enough" of something?
- How has God provided for you in the past?

Scriptures and Quotes

Are God's consolations not enough for you, words spoken gently to you?
Job 15:11

Even to your old age and gray hairs I am he, I am he who will sustain you. I have made you and I will carry you; I will sustain you and I will rescue you.
Isaiah 46:4

The Lord will guide you always; he will satisfy your needs in a sun-scorched land and will strengthen your frame.
Isaiah 58:11

*The L*ORD* is good, a refuge in times of trouble.*
He cares for those who trust in him.
NAHUM 1:7

And God is able to make all grace abound to you, so that in all things at
all times, having all that you need, you will abound in every good work.
2 CORINTHIANS 9:8

My grace is sufficient for you, for my power is made perfect in weakness.
2 CORINTHIANS 12:9

I know what it is to be in need, and I know what it is to have plenty.
I have learned the secret of being content in any and every situation,
whether well fed or hungry, whether living in plenty or in want. I can do
everything through him who gives me strength.
PHILIPPIANS 4:12–13

Command those who are rich in this present world not to be arrogant nor
to put their hope in wealth, which is so uncertain, but to put their hope in
God, who richly provides us with everything for our enjoyment.
1 TIMOTHY 6:17

Truly, one of the crowning discoveries—the last and greatest lesson that the
soul has to learn—is to know that God is enough.[55]
CYNTHIA HEALD

How often do we look upon God as our last and feeblest resource!
We go to Him because we have nowhere else to go. And then
we learn that the storms of life have driven us, not upon the
rocks, but into the desired haven.[56]
GEORGE MACDONALD

MEDITATION

How can we know God is enough? We can begin by
remembering who He is. There is only one true God. Our God is
the Creator of all. He is sovereign over all the world. He is almighty,
omniscient, all loving, and all-powerful. He is the great I AM who
was and is and is to come. He is our God.

We are also assured that God is enough when we think of all He has done for us over the course of our lives—how He met our needs and held us up during the hardest times, times we don't think we could have survived without Him. Looking back, we see how He interceded for us, how He worked all things together for our good—how He sustained us with His mercy and lifted us up by His grace.

Most of all, we know God is enough because He sacrificed His Son, Jesus Christ, to ensure we will have eternal life once we believe in Him. Through our salvation He adopted us as His sons and daughters. We who believe have access to the throne of God; we have the Holy Spirit dwelling within us, and we are heirs of all the blessings of heaven. What else could God do to prove how much He loves us and wants to have a relationship with us?

When we see disasters strike and people hurting, when we see the horrors of war and wonder why it seems that evil has been given full reign in our world, we can trust that God is enough. Because we live in a fallen world, there will always be trouble, but God promises never to leave us or forsake us. When He doesn't take away the trials, He is with us in them. We are His, created in His image, and He will hold us close until the day He brings us home to dwell with Him forever.

In times of pain or frustration, in times of confusion and doubt, before we exhaust all earthly solutions for our situation, we need to remember to trust in God. To take a deep breath and say, "God is enough." He will not disappoint us.

For Reflection or Discussion

- Can you recall a difficult time in your life when you know God intervened and got you through it?
- How can we know that God's hand is at work in our situations and circumstances?
- Where have you experienced God's sufficiency most recently?

A Thought to Share

When we are weak, God is strong. He is enough.

Suggestion for the Week

Ask God to reveal any part of your life where you've failed to believe He is enough. Then listen for His answer.

Suggested Hymns

- Great Is Thy Faithfulness
- He Giveth More Grace
- O God, Our Help in Ages Past

Prayer Requests and Closing Prayer

LESSON 40

Jesus Heals

KEY VERSE

People brought all their sick to him and begged him to let the sick just touch the edge of his cloak, and all who touched him were healed.
MATTHEW 14:35–36

OPENING PRAYER

O LORD, HOW DESPERATELY WE NEED Your healing touch. Whether we suffer from physical ailments or wounds of the heart and spirit, Lord, we know our best hope for healing, whether here or in eternity, is to bring everything that ails us to You. In Your name we pray, amen.

INTRODUCTION

Oh, the many efforts we go through to be healed of one malady or another. Our medicine cabinets may contain salves for bee stings or common rashes, pills to ease headaches and arthritis pains, as well as lifesaving medications controlling our blood pressure, keeping our thyroid at an operational level, or even regulating the rhythm of our heartbeats.

Some people even journey great distances in search of a cure. Eighty thousand ill or disabled people from many countries go to Lourdes, France, each year. They place their hope in the curing waters and light candles in the grotto where a young French woman reported having received messages from the Virgin Mary in 1858. There are numerous reported miracles of healing at Lourdes since that date, but there is no guarantee of a miracle for every visitor. Miracles do occur today throughout the world, yet desperate people have also been misled and disappointed by those who call themselves healers but can't deliver the promised cure.

The truth is that, try as we might to cure whatever ails us, the human body wasn't designed to last forever. Despite our best efforts and those of skilled physicians, eventually these earthly bodies we are sometimes blessed, sometimes cursed to possess will fail us. By that time, we may be as done with them as they are with us.

Not all our pains and ailments are physical in nature. Our spirits suffer too. The longer we live, the more likely we will have experienced devastating losses, heartbreak, disappointments, and maybe even abuse. We are in as much need of healing in these areas as in our bodies.

Yes, there's no lifetime guarantee on our earthly bodies, and no promise that all our heartaches will disappear. Nevertheless, there is assurance we will be eternally healed of all that ails us once we surrender ourselves—body, heart, mind, and soul—to Jesus Christ.

FOR REFLECTION OR DISCUSSION

- Do you rely on treatments or medications to stay healthy?
- Have you personally known of a healing miracle?
- How far would you be willing to go for a promised cure?

SCRIPTURES AND QUOTES

Praise the LORD, O my soul, and forget not all his benefits—who forgives all your sins and heals all your diseases.
PSALM 103:2–3

He heals the brokenhearted and binds up their wounds.
PSALM 147:3

But he was pierced for our transgressions, he was crushed for our iniquities; the punishment that brought us peace was upon him, and by his wounds we are healed.
ISAIAH 53:5

Heal me, O LORD, and I will be healed; save me and I will be saved, for you are the one I praise.
JEREMIAH 17:14

But for you who revere my name, the sun of righteousness will rise with healing in its wings. And you will go out and leap like calves released from the stall.
MALACHI 4:2

Jesus went throughout Galilee, teaching in their synagogues, preaching the good news of the kingdom, and healing every disease and sickness among the people.
MATTHEW 4:23

She said to herself, "If I only touch his cloak, I will be healed." Jesus turned and saw her. "Take heart, daughter," he said, "your faith has healed you." And the woman was healed from that moment.
MATTHEW 9:21–22

At the name of Jesus hell trembles and heaven sings. In no other name is salvation found or healing available.[57]
CYNDY SHERWOOD

Our infirmities become the black velvet on which the diamond of God's love glitters all the more brightly.[58]
CHARLES SPURGEON

MEDITATION

The New Testament of the Bible tells of the healing Jesus did while here on earth, and His methods were as varied as the people He helped. He healed a demon-possessed man by sending the demons into a herd of pigs (Mark 5:11–13). He healed a blind man by smearing mud on his eyes (John 9:6). He watched a paralytic be lowered through the roof of a house and then told him to arise and take his mat (Mark 2:3–4, 11). He felt the gentle touch of a woman who had an issue of bleeding for twelve years and healed her merely by acknowledging her faith in Him (Matthew 9:20–22). Jesus healed many people during his three-year ministry, but He didn't heal everyone and He still doesn't.

A man who had recently married a woman he adored and who adored him was injured in a bicycle accident on a mountain pass. From the moment he was airlifted to a hospital, he couldn't move his legs. After weeks in a rehab facility, his fate as a paraplegic seemed certain, yet he and his wife didn't give up. They claimed every verse about healing they could find in the Bible and prayed desperately for Jesus to do it again. They believed they would see His mercy and compassion in action. They held a prayer service where many believers and even the president of a seminary laid hands on the man. Yet, over twenty years later, he is still bound by his physical limitations and spends all his time in a wheelchair or in bed, being cared for by his wife and other caregivers.

This is a good man, a faithful man, a man who believes in the power of the risen Lord with all his heart, but he has not yet been healed. Will he be healed? Yes. When the time comes for him to join the Lord in heaven, he will be completely healed, and all the scripture promises he claims will be fulfilled.

We don't know why some are healed on this earth while others are not. Only the Great Physician knows. He may reveal His reasoning to us some day, or we may just learn to trust Him so explicitly we don't even question why when we see Him face-to-face. On that day, we will be *sown a natural body* and *raised a spiritual body* (1 Corinthians 15:44). Let's leap like calves released from the stall together!

For Reflection or Discussion

- Have you ever prayed for a healing that didn't come? How did that make you feel?
- Have you ever asked others to pray for your healing? Why or why not?
- What ailments do you look forward to leaving behind with your earthly body?

A Thought to Share

When you can't see His hand at work, trust His heart.

SUGGESTION FOR THE WEEK

If you have a physical or emotional ailment that needs healing this week, take it to Jesus believing He will heal you in His time. You don't even have to make an appointment or find transportation.

SUGGESTED HYMNS

- He Touched Me
- My Faith Has Found a Resting Place
- There Is a Balm in Gilead

PRAYER REQUESTS AND CLOSING PRAYER

LESSON 41

Fan the Flame

KEY VERSE

For this reason I remind you to fan into flame the gift of God, which is in you through the laying on of my hands. For God did not give us a spirit of timidity, but a spirit of power, of love and of self-discipline.
2 TIMOTHY 1:6–7

OPENING PRAYER

O LORD, HOW BLESSED WE ARE to have the Holy Spirit within us once we believe in Jesus Christ, Your Son. How grateful we are to receive Your spiritual gifts as well. Help us keep this flame of gifts burning brightly within us, Lord. For You promise it will never be snuffed out. In Jesus' name we pray, amen.

INTRODUCTION

No doubt most of us have some wonderful memories of fireplaces we've loved for their warmth and beauty. Places where we curled up in a chair nearby to read a book or warmed our hands after a walk outside in winter. Places where we laid children's socks and mittens to dry or patted a dog curled up on the hearth. Maybe some of us even remember cooking or popping popcorn over an open fire for a special family gathering.

Such marvelous wood fires take work, however. Chopping, stacking, and carrying wood were chores lots of us recall, as was scooping out the ashes into the ash bin. But all the work was worth it to have a crackling fire to enjoy long into the cold winter night.

Both Boy Scouts and Girl Scouts learn how to make a fire in the woods with a piece of flint and some dry twigs and pine needles. All it takes is one spark, and the first puff of a tiny fire comes to life. As it grows, bigger pieces of wood can be added until a glorious campfire glows where the young people can gather around to tell stories and sing songs. Oh, the memories made around such campfires—whether at a youth camp or on a family camping trip.

We fondly remember fires of the past, but do we spend enough time thinking about the fire burning within us? Do we fan the flame of our spiritual gifts, as Paul wrote to his protégée Timothy, or do we just let it dwindle? Rest assured there are things we can do, even at an older age, to use the gifts of the Spirit and keep them burning brightly within us—right up until God says our time on earth is done.

For Reflection or Discussion

- What fireplaces come to mind when you think of homes you've lived in or places you've visited?
- As a child, did you have chores related to the wood-burning fireplace or stove in your childhood home? What were they?
- Is there a fireplace you enjoy cozying up to in your life today?

Scriptures and Quotes

Create in me a pure heart, O God, and renew a steadfast spirit within me. Do not cast me from your presence or take your Holy Spirit from me. Restore to me the joy of your salvation and grant me a willing spirit, to sustain me.
Psalm 51:10–12

I baptize you with water for repentance. But after me will come one who is more powerful than I, whose sandals I am not fit to carry. He will baptize you with the Holy Spirit and with fire.
Matthew 3:11

But the Counselor, the Holy Spirit, whom the Father will send in my name, will teach you all things and will remind you of everything I have said to you.
JOHN 14:26

When the day of Pentecost came, they were all together in one place. Suddenly a sound like the blowing of a violent wind came from heaven and filled the whole house where they were sitting. They saw what seemed to be tongues of fire that separated and came to rest on each of them. All of them were filled with the Holy Spirit and began to speak in other tongues as the Spirit enabled them.
ACTS 2:1–4

We have different gifts, according to the grace given us. If a man's gift is prophesying, let him use it in proportion to his faith. If it is serving, let him serve; if it is teaching, let him teach; if it is encouraging, let him encourage; if it is contributing to the needs of others, let him give generously; if it is leadership, let him govern diligently; if it is showing mercy, let him do it cheerfully.
ROMANS 12:6–8

There are different kinds of gifts, but the same Spirit. There are different kinds of service, but the same Lord. There are different kinds of working, but the same God works all of them in all men.
1 CORINTHIANS 12:4–6

Each one should use whatever gift he has received to serve others, faithfully administering God's grace in its various forms.
1 PETER 4:10

Being born of the Spirit means much more than we generally take it to mean. It gives us a new vision and keeps us absolutely fresh for everything by the perennial supply of the life of God.[59]
OSWALD CHAMBERS

MEDITATION

Believers in Christ surely know the Holy Spirit has indwelled them from the moment they believed, but is it possible, as we age, even those of us who believe forget this indwelling gave us at least one spiritual gift and possibly more (Romans 12:6–8)?

Paul knew that young Timothy had been given the gift of teaching, maybe of leadership and shepherding as well. Theologians surmise, however, that Timothy may have been shy about using his gifts, so Paul encouraged him to be bold in his faith and to fan into flame the gift of God.

We need to be similarly encouraged. As we age, we can easily become complacent about using our spiritual gifts. (See Lesson 35 in *The Hope of Glory*, Volume One.) We may think the world no longer needs the gift we've been given by the Holy Spirit, but nothing could be further from the truth.

So how can we take a gift that's died down to a flicker, or is maybe no more than a glowing ember, and fan it into flame? We don't need bellows. First, we need to trust that the gift God gave us is still there. Then we must pray and ask Him to send the gentle breath of the Holy Spirit to fan our gift back into flame—even into a roaring fire!

For as long as we live, our gifts of encouragement, mercy, helps, administration, teaching, faith, and all the other gifts the Spirit bestows are desperately needed and easily accessed. We need only ask the Lord to fan our flame and give us the same spirit of power, of love, and of self-discipline that Paul exhorted Timothy to claim. Our gifts are needed. Let's let the Word of God, our faith, and prayer fan them into glorious flames that will provide light and warmth to our corner of the world.

FOR REFLECTION OR DISCUSSION

- The gifts of the Spirit are mentioned in 1 Corinthians 12:7–11; Romans 12:6–8; Ephesians 4:11–13; and 1 Peter 4:10–11. Do you know what your spiritual gifts are?
- From a small match flame to a roaring campfire, how strongly do you think the flame of your spiritual gifting is burning today?
- What could you do to fan the flame within you?

A Thought to Share

Let what shines in you on the inside show on the outside.

Suggestion for the Week

Now is not too late to learn your spiritual gifts. Some churches offer a tool you can use to reveal your gifting, but the discovery can be simpler also. Ask a believing friend whom you trust what gifts they see in you. Think about when you feel most alive and closest to God. That's probably when you are using your gifting.

Suggested Hymns

- Breathe on Me, Breath of God
- Spirit of the Living God
- This Little Light of Mine

Prayer Requests and Closing Prayer

Lesson 42

Merciful Heavens!

Key Verse

> *Oh, give thanks to the Lord, for He is good!*
> *For His mercy endures forever.*
> Psalm 136:1 (NKJV)

Opening Prayer

O Lord, where would we be without Your mercy? How grateful we are You save us from what we truly deserve. Your mercy reaches to the heavens, Lord, and it sustains us and keeps us safe in You. Thank You, Lord, for Your mercy. In Jesus' name, amen.

Introduction

Many of us may remember our mother exclaiming, "Merciful heavens!" This exclamation was delivered at high volume and was usually reserved for major disasters such as when she dropped the tuna casserole on the kitchen floor or found a run in her last good pair of hose. On occasion, it could even erupt after hearing good news, such as: "Sue Ann is pregnant with triplets!" "Merciful heavens!"

Bart Millard is the lead singer of the popular Christian contemporary band MercyMe. The group is best known for the song "I Can Only Imagine," which has helped many people who are grieving with its comforting message about what heaven might be like. The band got its name from a similar expression about mercy that Bart's grandmother used. When he was a young youth ministry intern working on developing his musical talents and writing songs, his grandmother was concerned that he seemed to always be at home when she called. "Mercy me!" she'd exclaim. "Why don't you get a real job?"

Mercy is more than an expression though. A clear definition is that mercy is not getting what we deserve, as opposed to grace, which is getting what we don't deserve. Another grandmother had this definition of mercy illustrated for her when she was driving out of town for her granddaughter's basketball game. Anxious to get to the game on time, she was driving above the speed limit and was pulled over by a traffic officer. After she explained the situation to the officer, he said, "Well, we want you to get to the game safely, ma'am. Please slow down."

That next Sunday at church the pastor asked if anyone had an example they could share of a time when they received mercy. The kindness of the police officer gave the grandma a perfect example to relate.

We appreciate the kindness when anyone extends mercy to us—a policeman with every right to give us a ticket, the grocery store clerk who waves us into the express lane even if we have too many items, or the friend who knows we didn't mean to forget to call them. Mercy me! We all need mercy. The mercy we need the most is that coming down to us from our merciful Father in heaven.

For Reflection or Discussion

- Can you remember a time when you were grateful for the mercy that someone extended to you?
- When have you been merciful to someone else?
- Have you ever thought about the difference between mercy and grace before?

Scriptures and Quotes

I will have mercy on whom I will have mercy, and I will have compassion on whom I will have compassion.
EXODUS 33:19

Surely goodness and mercy shall follow me all the days of my life: and I
will dwell in the house of the LORD for ever.
PSALM 23:6 (KJV)

Remember, O LORD, your great mercy and love, for they are from of old.
PSALM 25:6

Your mercy, O LORD, is in the heavens;
Your faithfulness reaches to the clouds.
PSALM 36:5 (NKJV)

O LORD, I say to you, "You are my God."
Hear, O LORD, my cry for mercy.
PSALM 140:6

And what does the LORD require of you? To act justly and to love mercy
and to walk humbly with your God.
MICAH 6:8

Blessed are the merciful, for they will be shown mercy.
MATTHEW 5:7

His mercy extends to those who fear him, from generation to generation.
LUKE 1:50

Praise be to the God and Father of our Lord Jesus Christ! In his
great mercy he has given us new birth into a living hope through the
resurrection of Jesus Christ from the dead.
1 PETER 1:3

Teach me to feel another's woe,
To hide the fault I see;
That mercy I to others show,
That mercy show to me.[60]
ALEXANDER POPE

MEDITATION

Mercy is listed as one of the spiritual gifts given to some believers
once they believe (Romans 12:8), so being merciful comes easier for
some of us than for others. Still, that doesn't mean we are to forgo

being merciful at all. When we are in the position of judging someone for a perceived wrong, can we choose mercy instead? *Mercy triumphs over judgment!* we read in James 2:13, so we should be merciful.

In newer translations of the Bible, the word mercy is often translated as love, compassion, or loving-kindness. Since we are all called upon to be loving, compassionate, and kind, we should all be able to dig deep into God's storehouse of resources for us and be merciful as well.

So often grace and mercy are mentioned together in the Bible, and what a blessed partnership they form. The Apostle Paul often began his letters with a greeting similar to the one he wrote to young Timothy: *Grace, mercy and peace from God the Father and Christ Jesus our Lord* (2 Timothy 1:2). Adding peace to the sisters of grace and mercy completes the picture of a perfect life in Christ, does it not?

In our humanity, we aren't always able to exude grace, mercy, and peace. Gratefully, God can do so, and of the three perhaps we should be most grateful for His mercy.

God showers every believer with His mercy daily, and most of the time we may not even be aware His merciful hand is at work. He even grants mercy to those who don't believe in Him because He loves all whom He has created. Yet He reserves His greatest gift of mercy for those who accept Jesus Christ as their Lord and Savior. We read in Romans 5:8: *But God demonstrates his own love for us in this: While we were still sinners, Christ died for us.*

Because of His great mercy, God wanted to make sure we could have a relationship with Him and dwell with Him for all eternity— so He sent His Son to die for our sins. He didn't wait for us to be perfect people or win awards for church attendance. Rather, while we were still sinners, He gave His most merciful gift. As we ponder how merciful God has been to us, let us be merciful to others.

FOR REFLECTION OR DISCUSSION

- Why do you think we sometimes find it difficult to show mercy to others?
- Is it easier to judge or be merciful?
- Could showing mercy lead to more forgiving, loving relationships? How?

A Thought to Share

Let mercy dance with a wide and swirling skirt.

Suggestion for the Week

Be alert to any amount of mercy sprinkled into your life this week, then shower someone with more.

Suggested Hymns

- Great Is Thy Faithfulness
- There's a Wideness in God's Mercy
- To God Be the Glory

Prayer Requests and Closing Prayer

LESSON 43

Gladly We Come

KEY VERSE

Worship the LORD with gladness; come before him with joyful songs.
PSALM 100:2

OPENING PRAYER

O LORD, SO MANY THINGS THAT happen to us in this life can make our hearts heavy and sad. But when we think of You and all You are, we worship You with gladness! Thank You, Lord, that this very act lifts our hearts. Gladly we come to You. In Jesus' name, amen.

INTRODUCTION

What does it take for us to feel glad? How does gladness differ from happiness? The makers of Glad® household products air commercials trying to convince us that if only we have garbage bags that don't tear open and leak or sandwich bags that seal securely, we will be glad. But is that really all it takes to make us glad?

Happiness and gladness are similar emotions, but there is a difference. When we are happy, we are in a sustained state of contentment, as in "She is a happy person," or "He lived a happy life." In contrast, we are more likely to exclaim, "Oh, I'm so glad!" when something turns out the way we hoped or we are satisfied with our immediate circumstances. In other words, gladness is more often an instant feeling linked with a certain trigger for being pleased or content.

Examples? A young woman might be *happy* that she is engaged to a man she loves and will be getting married soon. She is *glad* when she receives a phone call telling her that her first choice of venue for the wedding is available on the date she prefers. An older woman may be *happy* that she is able to take a trip to a location affording her the opportunity to see the amazing Northern Lights, the Aurora Borealis. But she will be *glad* the moment those colorful, dancing beams appear in the night sky.

Surely most of us are content to feel either happy or glad, right? But the fact that so many Bible verses mention feeling glad or being filled with gladness tells us we should never merely be complacently content with who God is or with the truth of the gospel. No, every time we think of all God has done for us, we should feel glad and worship Him with gladness.

FOR REFLECTION OR DISCUSSION

- Is there an event in nature you are always glad to see?
- What piece of news last had you exclaiming, "I'm so glad"?
- Have you ever thought about the difference between happiness and gladness?

SCRIPTURES AND QUOTES

Let the heavens rejoice, let the earth be glad; let them say among the nations, "The LORD reigns!"
1 CHRONICLES 16:31

Satisfy us in the morning with your unfailing love, that we may sing for joy and be glad all our days.
PSALM 90:14

This is the day which the LORD hath made; we will rejoice and be glad in it.
PSALM 118:24 (KJV)

I was glad when they said unto me, Let us go into the house of the LORD.
PSALM 122:1 (KJV)

The Spirit of the Sovereign LORD is on me, because the LORD has anointed me to preach good news to the poor . . . to comfort all who mourn, and provide for those who grieve in Zion—to bestow on them a crown of beauty instead of ashes, the oil of gladness instead of mourning.
ISAIAH 61:1, 2–3

Then maidens will dance and be glad, young men and old as well. I will turn their mourning into gladness; I will give them comfort and joy instead of sorrow.
JEREMIAH 31:13

Rejoice and be glad, because great is your reward in heaven.
MATTHEW 5:12

Let us rejoice and be glad and give him glory! For the wedding of the Lamb has come, and his bride has made herself ready.
REVELATION 19:7

Because the Lord has made this day, we can look past the closed doors to see people and opportunities we had previously overlooked. In celebrating their value, we will discover joy and gladness from God.[61]
DAVID C. MCCASLAND

MEDITATION

What better way to start each day than to recite Psalm 118:24 (KJV): *This is the day which the LORD hath made; we will rejoice and be glad in it.* There are so many messages for us in that one verse. First, the verse inspires a sense of gratitude that we have been given a new day. Each day is a gift from God waiting to be unwrapped, and the psalmist reminds us of that. Second, this new day is in the Lord's hands. He has ordained it for us, and He knows what the new day will bring. We can trust Him with each day we live. Once we take those truths to heart, certainly we can enter the day with a spirit of gladness.

Yet there are times when we must search for the gladness in a day, aren't there? When someone we love dies and we are so sad we don't know if we can even get out of bed, the things that make us glad may be few and far between. That's when we need to remember that God made even that sad day, and there is gladness to be found even in the midst of our circumstances when we look for it through eyes of faith.

Isaiah was the most respected prophet of his time and began his ministry in 740 BC. He is often described as "the greatest writing prophet." Because the Spirit of the Lord was upon him and he was anointed to preach good news, Isaiah had much to say about the restoration and redemption of the people of Judea. Yet much of what he wrote was not only true for those people but proved to be prophetic, preparing the way for the greater restoration and redemption the coming Messiah would bring.

When we read in Isaiah that he came to bestow *the oil of gladness instead of mourning* (Isaiah 61:3), we are reminded Jesus came to do that as well—but even more effectively. We may not be physically anointed with oil to bless us, as was the practice in Isaiah's time, but we do feel the healing balm Jesus brings into our mourning and sadness. The anointing with oil was reserved for joyous occasions. Always we can rejoice in Him! Always we can be glad.

FOR REFLECTION OR DISCUSSION

- How can we worship the Lord with gladness as it says in our key verse?
- Have you ever been aware of gladness in the midst of sadness?
- Have you been anointed with oil in a physical or symbolic sense?

A THOUGHT TO SHARE

To be filled with gladness, worship gladly.

SUGGESTION FOR THE WEEK

It's possible to add some gladness to someone else's life. Share some good news with someone. Especially the good news of the gospel message.

Suggested Hymns

- Day by Day—A Prayer
- The Lord's Prayer
- This Is the Day

Prayer Requests and Closing Prayer

LESSON 44

We Are One

KEY VERSE

All the believers were one in heart and mind.
ACTS 4:32

OPENING PRAYER

O LORD, HOW IT MUST GRIEVE You to see Your children divided and bickering. We pray, whatever dissension there is in the world, there will always be unity among believers. We pray what unites us will be stronger than what divides us. Make us one, Lord. In Jesus' name, amen.

INTRODUCTION

Our country is severely divided. Although our Pledge of Allegiance states we are "One nation under God," and we still claim to believe "United we stand and divided we fall," the chasms of division often seem too broad for a bridge to span them. But among believers, Christ is that bridge.

Two women who found a way to agree to disagree in unity and love wrote a book together in hopes it would inspire others to get along. They hoped that, even when people couldn't come to a point of agreement or even compromise, they would still be able to treat one another with dignity and respect.

The book was titled *Reconcilable Differences: Two Friends Debate God's Roles for Women*, although the coauthors would have preferred their initial title for the book, *How Can She Believe That?*[62] One coauthor described herself as an egalitarian, believing women should fill any role in the church. The other coauthor described herself as a complementarian, believing that God asks men to lead His church but gives women equally important roles to play.

The two friends often had heated debates in the writing of the book, but from the beginning they were determined not to let their disagreements affect their friendship. They knew they would see one another in heaven and so wanted to learn to get along here on earth. At the end of each chapter, they cowrote a statement of unity highlighting the points on which they could agree. Their friendship survived and thrived.

What happened to the ability to agree to disagree in a spirit of love and respect? What happened to politicians of either party being able to work together for the common good? What happened to civil discourse in our society?

As believers in Jesus Christ, we are never asked to compromise the truth of the gospel. We are never to veer away from God's inerrant Word, the Holy Bible. Within our circles of influence, and especially within the church, we are called to be unifiers, not dividers. We are called to be one body, united in heart and mind. All for the glory of God.

For Reflection or Discussion

- Have you ever had a heated disagreement with a friend? How did it turn out?
- Why do you think it's difficult for people to agree to disagree while keeping their relationship intact?
- How can we be unifiers in the world in which we live or within the community of believers?

Scriptures and Quotes

How good and pleasant it is when God's people live together in unity!
PSALM 133:1 (NIV, 2011)

So in Christ we who are many form one body,
and each member belongs to all the others.
ROMANS 12:5

May the God who gives endurance and encouragement give you a spirit of
unity among yourselves as you follow Christ Jesus, so that with one heart
and mouth you may glorify the God and Father of our Lord Jesus Christ.
ROMANS 15:5–6

For we were all baptized by one Spirit into one body—whether Jews or
Greeks, slave or free—and we were all given the one Spirit to drink.
1 CORINTHIANS 12:13

There is one body and one Spirit—just as you were called to one hope
when you were called—one Lord, one faith, one baptism; one God and
Father of all, who is over all and through all and in all.
EPHESIANS 4:4–6

Make my joy complete by being like-minded,
having the same love, being one in spirit and purpose.
PHILIPPIANS 2:2

This might surprise you, but it is entirely possible to have differences and
still love someone. Jesus did it all the time.[63]
CYNDY SHERWOOD

MEDITATION

The ministry of Jesus Christ on earth spanned three short years. After all the profound messages He delivered, all the people healed and miracles performed, He knew His earthly assignment was drawing to a close. The night before He was crucified, He walked away from the others to pray to His heavenly Father in the Garden of Gethsemane. What was on His heart that dark night? We were.

The prayer Jesus prayed is recorded for us in John 17, and what a gift it is to anyone who needs assurance he or she is loved. As He knelt in obedience and despair, Jesus implored His Father in heaven to give His disciples—and all who would believe because of the gospel message they would share—unity, protection, and sanctification. Here, we focus on His plea for unity among believers.

Jesus knew His disciples were not alike. They were individuals with different temperaments and experiences, just as believers are today. Yet He also knew for the purposes of the kingdom of God, for the spread of the gospel, they would have to work together—to be like-minded and of one heart. They needed to be unified for the mission to succeed.

In John 17:11, Jesus prayed, *"Holy Father, protect them by the power of your name—the name you gave me—so that they may be one as we are one."*

From what did He know we would need to be protected? From our selfish desires to have our own way. From the distractions Satan would throw at us in an attempt to get us to argue over the style of our worship music or what color the church carpeting should be—not to mention more serious, yet nonessential, doctrinal issues.

Jesus continued praying as drops of blood fell like sweat from Him. In John 17:22–23, He prayed, *"I have given them the glory that you gave me, that they may be one as we are one: I in them and you in me. May they be brought to complete unity to let the world know that you sent me and have loved them even as you have loved me."*

As with much of the Bible's teaching, a high standard is set. Complete unity may be difficult to achieve. But because we are loved, each of us can do his or her part to be one with other believers. The impact of the gospel message depends on it.

For Reflection or Discussion

- Have you ever had to give up a personal preference to uphold the unity of the Body of Christ?
- Are there any issues in your mind or heart that divide you from other believers now?
- Why is the unity of believers important to the kingdom of God and His work on this earth?

A Thought to Share

There is more that unites us than divides us.

Suggestion for the Week

If you have a disagreement with someone this week, see if you can turn the discussion in a direction of unity, love, and respect—even if you still can't agree.

Suggested Hymns

- Blest Be the Tie That Binds
- The Church's One Foundation
- We Are One in the Spirit (Contemporary)

Prayer Requests and Closing Prayer

LESSON 45

God Is Our Help

KEY VERSE

Because you are my help, I sing in the shadow of your wings.
PSALM 63:7

OPENING PRAYER

O GOD, HOW OFTEN WE NEED Your help. No matter what circumstance we find ourselves in, we know we need only call out to You and You will be able and willing to help us. Thank You, Almighty One, for coming to our aid. In Jesus' name, amen.

INTRODUCTION

Our society would be in deep trouble without our first responders, wouldn't it? Police officers, firefighters, and EMTs all provide such valuable help when it's needed, and all we have to do to get their help is call 9-1-1 and wait.

No example of the heroism of such first responders is as ingrained in our memories as the response rendered on September 11, 2001. After planes hijacked by terrorists crashed into both towers of the World Trade Center in New York City, occupants of the buildings were desperate to escape the burning infernos, some so desperate they jumped to their deaths rather than be burned alive.

While thousands of people raced down stairwells in an attempt to get out of the buildings before they collapsed, brave New York City police officers and firemen in full gear raced up the stairs in an attempt to save as many as possible. The definition of a hero is the willingness to sacrifice one's own life for the lives of others. Those men and women were our heroes that day.

Most of us know when it's time to call in the first responders, but are we as astute in knowing when to ask for help in nonemergency situations? If we need help getting to a doctor's appointment, do we ask for it or miss the appointment? If we need help reconciling a relationship with a loved one, do we ask for it or just hope things will get better in time?

A three-year-old girl was struggling to put her ballet slippers on for a class she was taking. Her mom said, "Here, let me help you." The pretty little child, her blonde hair pulled back in a ballerina bun, looked up at her mom and assertively said, "No. I can do it myself."

We smile when we think of this precious one's need to establish independence from her mom and to gain confidence in her own abilities. Yet there are times when we all need help. God no doubt watches us, His precious children, struggle with life at times and wonders why we are so stubborn and independent—why we don't ask for His help when we need it.

For Reflection or Discussion

- Have you ever had to call 9-1-1 in an emergency? What happened?
- Is there an area of your life today where you need help but are refusing to ask for it?
- Why do you think we are so reluctant to ask others for help?

Scriptures and Quotes

Listen to my cry for help, my King and my God, for to you I pray.
PSALM 5:2

Be pleased, O LORD, to save me; O LORD, come quickly to help me.
PSALM 40:13

God is our refuge and strength, an ever-present help in trouble.
PSALM 46:1

I lift up my eyes to the hills—where does my help come from? My help comes from the LORD, the Maker of heaven and earth.
PSALM 121:1–2

The widow who is really in need and left all alone puts her hope in God and continues night and day to pray and to ask God for help.
1 TIMOTHY 5:5

Let us then approach the throne of grace with confidence, so that we may receive mercy and find grace to help us in our time of need.
HEBREWS 4:16

God's help is only a prayer away.
ANONYMOUS

MEDITATION

The Bible is full of events where God intervened to render help when it was needed. Without God's help, Moses wouldn't have been able to lead his people out of Egypt and through the Red Sea safely. Without God's help, David wouldn't have been able to slay Goliath armed with only his slingshot and a smooth stone from the creek. If God can help an old man with a walking stick part the Red Sea and a young shepherd boy with no advanced weaponry defeat a giant, don't you think He might be able to help you?

A man who was sharing his testimony with a group of people recalled how he first came to learn about God at a summer camp before going away to college. Once he got to college that fall, however, he was homesick and lonely. Having so recently heard about the power of prayer he decided to give it a try.

"Lord," he prayed, "I'm so lonely. I don't know what You can do about it but I just wanted You to know. Please help me." Within five minutes of his prayer two things happened. First, he received a phone call from a friend he thought had long forgotten him. After hanging up the phone he heard a motorcycle pull up outside his dorm and looked out to see another long-lost friend who just decided to drop by to see how he was doing. God got his attention that day, and he hasn't stopped praying and believing since.

What's the common truth in all these accounts? The people who received God's help acknowledged they needed it. They knew they couldn't change the situation they faced without God's help. So, they asked Him to intervene.

While we wrestle with our personal situations, God patiently waits for us to ask for His help. We know from the scripture verses we just read, and from so many more in the Bible, He has both the power and the will to help us. Our bodies may fail us, our resources may run dry, but God is ever present and ever willing to be our help. In Isaiah 41:13, He says: *"For I am the LORD, your God, who takes hold of your right hand and says to you, Do not fear; I will help you."* Believe God will do what He promises. Ask for His help.

FOR REFLECTION OR DISCUSSION

- Can you recall a time when you asked for God's help and got it?
- How are we to respond when we ask God for help, but it doesn't seem like He is coming to our aid?
- In what ways can we allow God to help others through us?

A THOUGHT TO SHARE

Don't go to God only when you need help,
but always go to Him when you do.

SUGGESTION FOR THE WEEK

Identify one issue in your life where you feel you could use God's help. Give it over to Him in prayer every day this week and see what happens. Begin your prayer with three simple, powerful words: God, help me.

SUGGESTED HYMNS

- A Mighty Fortress is Our God
- Nearer My God, to Thee

PRAYER REQUESTS AND CLOSING PRAYER

LESSON 46

Generation to Generation

KEY VERSE

For the LORD is good and his love endures forever; his faithfulness
continues through all generations.
PSALM 100:5

OPENING PRAYER

O LORD, WE KNOW YOU PLACED each one of us in a specific generation for a purpose. Ours is one of the many generations You have blessed, protected, and allowed to thrive. Lord, we also know we are an important link between the generation before us and the ones that follow. Keep us mindful of our responsibility to serve well those who follow us. In Jesus' name, amen.

INTRODUCTION

A woman who was researching her family genealogy came across a French Bible that had been given to her great-grandmother as a child. As she carefully thumbed through the yellowed pages, she came across a small white feather with a red tip. It touched her so deeply to realize her great-grandmother had found that feather and tucked it in her Bible, never knowing her great-granddaughter would one day find it and consider it a true treasure.

The same woman also inherited an antique bed that had been her great-grandmother's. She was excited when two of her granddaughters were old enough to sleep in the bed on one of their visits. "My great-grandmother had eight babies in that bed," she explained. As she left the bedroom, she overheard one of the little girls ask her mother, "Did anyone wash the sheets?"

Grandkids delight us as almost no one else can. Most grandparents are quick to pull out their wallets or cell phones to share recent photos of grandchildren with anyone who expresses even the slightest interest. If we are blessed to spend time with our grandchildren, we feel like God is giving us a second chance to love unconditionally and to instruct carefully. The bond between grandparent and grandchild is uncomplicated by all the parameters of parenting. As the saying goes, we get to spoil them and send them home.

But is that enough? If we're blessed to be grandparents and great-grandparents, to be an important link in a family's overall history, don't we have a responsibility to tell of generations before us and invest our time, and maybe our resources, in generations that follow? Most of all, if we know Jesus as our personal Lord and Savior, shouldn't we share stories of His faithfulness with those in the generations that follow ours?

Being a part of God's plan for families is a wonderful gift, one we should never take for granted whether we are blessed to be grandparents or not.

For Reflection or Discussion

- Grandkids say some funny things. Can you recall a funny story to share?
- If you do not have grandchildren of your own, what other contact do you have with those in younger generations?
- Have you ever shared the story of your salvation and God's love with young relatives or young friends?

Scriptures and Quotes

Know therefore that the LORD your God is God; he is the faithful God, keeping his covenant of love to a thousand generations of those who love him and keep his commands.
DEUTERONOMY 7:9

But the plans of the LORD stand firm forever, the purposes of his heart through all generations.
PSALM 33:11

Even when I am old and gray, do not forsake me, O God, till I declare your power to the next generation, your might to all who are to come.
PSALM 71:18

We will tell the next generation the praiseworthy deeds of the LORD, his power, and the wonders he has done.
PSALM 78:4

Then we your people, the sheep of your pasture, will praise you forever; from generation to generation we will recount your praise.
PSALM 79:13

Lord, you have been our dwelling place throughout all generations.
PSALM 90:1

Tell it to your children, and let your children tell it to their children, and their children to the next generation.
JOEL 1:3

Now to him who is able to do immeasurably more than all we ask or imagine . . . to him be glory in the church and in Christ Jesus throughout all generations, for ever and ever! Amen.
EPHESIANS 3:20–21

We sense that to fulfill our life we now are called to . . . give to others so that when we leave this world, we can be what we have given.[64]
HENRI J. M. NOUWEN

MEDITATION

God doesn't have a favorite generation. Sometimes we are tempted to think God was closer to His people in days gone by, when we were younger, but perhaps our generation was closer to Him. Since God is the same yesterday, and today, and forever, His plan for generations is as strong and alive today as it was the day that He made a covenant with Abraham and told him, *"I will establish my covenant as an everlasting covenant between me and you and your descendants after you for the generations to come, to be your God and the God of your descendants after you*" (Genesis 17:7).

The same God was the God of our great-grandparents' generation and is the God of our generation and all the generations to follow ours. When we know Him and trust Him, that fact should give us great comfort.

It often strengthens our own faith to learn those who came before us knew God and had a strong faith too. To find a pastor in the family tree along with the scoundrels and pirates makes genealogists smile. Yet we don't automatically inherit the faith of our ancestors, and we can't force our own faith on our children and grandchildren. Only the Holy Spirit can lift the veil for them and give them a complete understanding of who God is and how He gave His Son to ensure we would have eternal life with Him. But we can pray for them, and we can share what our God and theirs has done for us.

As we reach our later years, it's normal for us to begin to wonder what legacy we will leave for others. Sometimes we feel like our family isn't interested in us—our life history, our experiences, or our beliefs. We need to fight through those feelings of rejection and look for even small opportunities to sprinkle the lives of those who follow us with the stardust of hope, of love, and of faith.

What we will leave behind is so much more than any wealth or material goods we may have accrued by God's grace. Our lasting gift is the story of who we are, how God protected us and guided us, and the encouraging message that our God will be their God, too, if they will just welcome Him into their generation. If we are to be what we give, we need to resist withdrawing from family and watch for any opportunity to give light and life.

For Reflection or Discussion

- Are you aware of any seeds of faith in your family tree?
- Have you ever had the opportunity to share your faith with a younger member of your family? How was that received?
- What could you still do to share what God has done for you with those younger than you are?

A Thought to Share

Grandchildren are a grandparent's link to the future.
Grandparents are the grandchild's link to the past.

Suggestion for the Week

Spend some quiet time making a list of significant faith milestones in your life. Choose one or more to share the next time you have the opportunity.

Suggested Hymns

- Faith of Our Fathers
- Great is Thy Faithfulness
- O God, Our Help in Ages Past

Prayer Requests and Closing Prayer

What Prayer Can Do

Key Verse

*This is the confidence we have in approaching God: that if we ask
anything according to his will, he hears us.*
1 John 5:14

Opening Prayer

Lord God, how blessed we are to be able to open our hearts to
You in prayer any time, night or day, knowing You will always hear
us and answer according to what You know is best for us. May we
remember to pray for Your will to be done, Lord, and not our own. In
Jesus' name, amen.

Introduction

The subject of prayer has inspired a plethora of articles, sermons,
and books by noted theologians and scholars throughout the centuries.
The beauty of it is that, much like faith, prayer is most pure, most easily
grasped, employed, and appreciated, in its simplest form.

How delighted God must be when He receives a simple, heartfelt
prayer like these from innocent, believing children:

Dear God, please send a new baby for mommy. The baby you
sent last week cries too much. Debbie, 7

Dear Lord: Thank you for the nice day today. You even fooled the
TV weatherman. Hank, 7

Dear Lord: Tomorrow is my birthday. Could you please put a
rainbow in the sky? Susan, 9

Knowing the Lord hears and treasures these prayers should make us feel better about any of our feeble attempts to make our requests known to the Lord on high, right? Whether we pray structured, formal prayers or just whisper "Jesus, help me" in a moment of desperation, all our prayers are heard and honored by Him.

Yet prayer is more than a wish list. Praying is a privilege we have to praise and communicate with the Almighty God. He may decide to honor our request for a better job, the healing of an illness, or a victory for our team. Maybe, maybe not. But we are promised that when we pray and ask according to His will, He will act for sure—now or in eternity. Coming to Him in prayer is something we should remember to do sooner rather than later because not until we pray can we begin to see what prayer can do.

For Reflection or Discussion

- Is prayer a part of your daily life?
- When and where do you tend to pray the most?
- How can we be sure our prayers are not just "wish lists"?

Scriptures and Quotes

If my people, who are called by my name, will humble themselves and pray and seek my face and turn from their wicked ways, then will I hear from heaven and will forgive their sin and will heal their land.
2 Chronicles 7:14

The Lord has heard my cry for mercy; the Lord accepts my prayer.
Psalm 6:9

Praise be to God, who has not rejected my prayer or withheld his love from me!
Psalm 66:20

May my prayer be set before you like incense; may the lifting up of my hands be like the evening sacrifice.
Psalm 141:2

Therefore I tell you, whatever you ask for in prayer, believe that you have received it, and it will be yours.
MARK 11:24

Do not be anxious about anything, but in everything, by prayer and petition, with thanksgiving, present your requests to God. And the peace of God, which transcends all understanding, will guard your hearts and your minds in Christ Jesus.
PHILIPPIANS 4:6–7

Devote yourselves to prayer, being watchful and thankful.
COLOSSIANS 4:2

And the prayer offered in faith will make the sick person well; the Lord will raise him up. If he has sinned, he will be forgiven.
JAMES 5:15

And they were holding golden bowls full of incense, which are the prayers of the saints.
REVELATION 5:8

Wondrously and mysteriously God moves from the periphery of our prayer experience to the center. A conversion of the heart takes place, a transformation of the spirit.[65]
RICHARD J. FOSTER

MEDITATION

Prayer is powerful. From the scripture verses we just read we can come up with a list of amazing things prayer can do. To begin, prayer can bring acceptance, forgiveness, healing, and freedom from anxiety. It can even bring miracles to pass.

An awe-inspiring story in 1 Kings 18:20–39 demonstrates the power of prayer. The prophet Elijah challenged the Baal worshippers to see whose God was stronger. He proposed they prepare a sacrifice on Mt. Carmel and ask Baal to answer their prayers with fire and burn up the sacrifice. Three times the followers of Baal cried out to their god, but nothing happened.

But then the prophet Elijah stepped forward and prayed: *"O Lord, God of Abraham, Isaac and Israel, let it be known today that you are God in Israel and that I am your servant and have done all these things at your command. Answer me, O Lord, answer me, so these people will know that you, O Lord, are God, and that you are turning their hearts back again"* (1 Kings 18:36–37*).

Once Elijah prayed, the one true God sent down so much fire that it burned up the sacrifice, the wood, the stones, the soil, and even licked up all the rain in the trench that fell in place of fire when the Baal worshippers cried out in vain. *When all the people saw this, they fell prostrate and cried, "The Lord—he is God! The Lord—he is God!"* (1 Kings 18:39).

We should also cry out in praise when we see what prayer can do for us. When we pray, we are lifted out of the mire of our human circumstances and begin to see our situation from God's perspective—with kingdom eyes. Prayer empties us of all the clutter in our hearts, minds, and souls so the Holy Spirit can fill us again with God's truth, mercy, and grace. That's what prayer can do for us.

What do our prayers do for God? He desires a relationship with us, and prayer brings us into His presence. Prayer allows Him to receive our praise and our attention and to release His will into our world when we pray for that which He promises to provide: things like wisdom, hope, strength, and peace. Our prayers are like sacrificial incense to Him—so precious they are gathered in golden bowls in heaven (Revelation 5:8).

When we pray and give our burdens to God, we can trust He is actively working on the situation, or He's working on us. Either way, praying builds our faith. Those who pray often stand amazed at all prayer can do.

For Reflection or Discussion

- What is your response if God doesn't seem to be answering your prayers?
- Do you think there's value in praying for something even if you never know how that prayer is answered?
- Why do you think praying to God transforms us?

A Thought to Share

Prayer may not change our situation, but it always changes us.

Suggestion for the Week

When in doubt about what to pray this week, pray the prayer that never fails: "Lord, Your will be done."

Suggested Hymns

- In the Garden
- Sweet Hour of Prayer

Prayer Requests and Closing Prayer

LESSON 48

Faithful Friends

KEY VERSE

A friend loves at all times.
PROVERBS 17:17

OPENING PRAYER

O LORD, IF ONLY WE COULD be the kind of friend to others that You are to us. Teach us how to be faithful, encouraging, dependable, and always available like You are. Teach us to love our friends sacrificially as You love us. In Your name we pray, amen.

INTRODUCTION

The hand of friendship we extend to another means so much more when God's love goes along with it. When friendship and love work together, it's as if we are wrapping a warm quilt of encouragement around others. Our actions are the squares in that quilt, and love is the thread that connects them.

You may not realize how often your acts of friendship have just enough love in them to turn them into quilts of encouragement, but they do. It's the little things you do that make the difference. For example, out of friendship you may pick up the phone to call a friend who's depressed. Out of love, you stay on the phone longer than you intended because you sense your friend needs to talk. How else might love enhance friendship?

Friendship listens. Love resists the temptation to give advice. Sometimes as helpful as we think our advice might be, our friend may not be able to hear it right away or may not be ready to accept it. Love tells us when to speak and when to listen.

Friendship forgives a wrong. Love forgets it. How encouraging it is when we apologize to a friend for our thoughtlessness only to discover that not only has she forgiven us, she doesn't even remember what we did. That's friendship and love in action.

Friendship makes a plan. Love is ready to roll with whatever changes happen along the way. A friend who is grieving may say she wants to get together but then realizes she just isn't up to it that day. A friend who loves understands the change in plans without question.

We can be a friend who reaches out in love because God first loved us (1 John 4:19). To be a friend who also loves others, we must rely on the power of the Father, the Son, and the Holy Spirit. Especially the Son, Jesus Christ, who showed us here on earth how to be a friend to others and even called us His friends.

For Reflection or Discussion

- Can you recall a time in your life when a friend wrapped you in a quilt of encouragement when you needed it most?
- To whom have you been blessed to be a friend lately?
- How does adding love to our friendship make it more meaningful?

Scriptures and Quotes

A man of many companions may come to ruin, but there is a friend who sticks closer than a brother.
Proverbs 18:24

Do to others as you would have them do to you.
Luke 6:31

Greater love has no one than this, that he lay down his life for his friends. You are my friends if you do what I command.
John 15:13–14

Therefore encourage one another and build each other up,
just as in fact you are doing.
1 THESSALONIANS 5:11

Do not forget to entertain strangers, for by so doing some people have
entertained angels without knowing it.
HEBREWS 13:2

Dear friends, since God so loved us, we also ought to love one another.
1 JOHN 4:11

Friendship is a bridge between two hearts.
ANONYMOUS

God evidently does not intend us all to be rich, or powerful or great, but
He does intend us all to be friends.
RALPH WALDO EMERSON

He loves to be in our company, as hard as that is for us to fathom, and to
be company to us. He didn't need disciples. He could have accomplished
every task He desired without them. He chose the disciples to have "part
with Him" (John 13:8), to partner with Him (2 Corinthians 6:1).[66]
BETH MOORE

MEDITATION

We all love thinking Jesus wants to be our friend, but have we thought about the fact that Jesus, in His humanity as the Son of Man, needed friends too? He could have traveled, taught the masses, and performed miracles without having His disciples with Him, but He preferred to have them along as friends to share in His amazing ministry.

We know why that would be more desirable, don't we? As insignificant as it is compared to Jesus' ministry, we even enjoy going to the movies more if we have one or more friends to watch it with us. Then we can see one another's reactions and discuss the finer points of the plot afterwards. It's a more complete experience.

Just as our friends may forget to show up for the movie or promise to call but let the day go by without doing so, Jesus' friends were sometimes a disappointment to Him too. The example we recall most vividly is when Jesus went to the Garden of Gethsemane to pray the night before His crucifixion. In Mark 14:34 we read that He asked the disciples, *"Stay here and keep watch."* Then He withdrew a short distance to pray. When He returned, the disciples were sleeping and Jesus said, *"Could you not keep watch for one hour? Watch and pray so you will not fall into temptation"* (Mark 14:37–38). Twice more He left them to pray, and twice more He came back to find them sleeping. Ultimately, the time for prayer and sleep was over. He said, *"Rise! Let us go! Here comes my betrayer!"* (Mark14:42).

So not only did the disciples, the closest friends of Jesus, fall asleep after He asked them to stand watch, ultimately Judas would betray Him and Peter would deny Him. Others hid in fear. His friends disappointed Him, but throughout the Gospels we find verses assuring us that Jesus still loved them unconditionally and forgave them completely. *"I have called you friends,"* Jesus said in John 15:15, *"for everything that I learned from my Father I have made known to you."*

We are Jesus' friends also once we believe in Him and follow Him. And He is a friend who cares for us. A friend who never leaves us or gives up on us, even if we disappoint Him. The most faithful friend we will ever know.

For Reflection or Discussion

- Why do you think life's experiences are richer in the company of friends?
- Can you say of Jesus, "He is a friend of mine?"
- How has He shown You that He is your faithful friend?

A Thought to Share

Strangers may be dear friends we just haven't met yet.

Suggestion for the Week

Make a new friend by being a friend. Observe a need someone else has and meet it. Eventually, you can add love to your new friendship.

Suggested Hymns

- Blest Be the Tie That Binds
- What a Friend We Have in Jesus

Prayer Requests and Closing Prayer

LESSON 49

Leaving the Past Behind

KEY VERSE

Forgetting what is behind and straining toward what is ahead,
I press on toward the goal to win the prize for which God
has called me heavenward in Christ Jesus.
PHILIPPIANS 3:13–14

OPENING PRAYER

O LORD, HOW GRATEFUL WE ARE when we look back and see how You have led us, protected us, and loved us in the past. But, Lord, as we age, please keep us from getting stuck in the past. Keep us looking forward, Lord, always anxious to see the next thing You do. In Jesus' name we pray, amen.

INTRODUCTION

Ah, the good old days. The older we get, the more days we have to look back on and the more likely we are to remember the good in each one and overlook the bad. It's wonderful to have fond memories of days gone by and to remember the lessons learned and people loved in days passed. But if we stay stuck in the past, we will miss everything the present and the future have to offer.

Does anyone remember the story of Miss Havisham? She was the character in the classic novel by Charles Dickens, *Great Expectations*. Miss Havisham's groom left her at the altar on her wedding day. She was never able to move on from that point in time. She wore her wedding dress for the rest of her life, and in film adaptations of the novel, her home becomes increasingly dark and spooky—with even an old wedding cake left to rot in one corner. According to Dickens, Miss Havisham was in her early thirties as the novel begins, but due to seclusion and bitterness, she aged very quickly.

There may be a bit of Miss Havisham in each of us. We do change clothes, although we may hold on to a favorite item of clothing well after it's out of date, but are there attitudes or biases we leave unchanged? Is it possible we have an experience so traumatic, or even so wonderful, that we refuse to move forward from that point in time?

Reflecting on the good things in our past can bring us joy and comfort, but getting stuck in the past may eventually keep us from living life fully to the end of our days. As long as we wake up in the morning and have breath in our lungs, God isn't finished with us. He has more to show us, more to teach us, more for us to do for the benefit of others and to bring Him glory here on earth. Let's accept the challenge to look to the future and not sit in the dark eating old wedding cake.

For Reflection or Discussion

- When you think of the good old days, what good things come to mind?
- What wasn't so good about the good old days?
- How can we keep from getting stuck in the past?

Scriptures and Quotes

This is the day the LORD has made; let us rejoice and be glad in it.
PSALM 118:24

Forget the former things; do not dwell on the past. See, I am doing a new thing! Now it springs up; do you not perceive it? I am making a way in the desert and streams in the wasteland.
ISAIAH 43:18–19

Behold, I will create new heavens and a new earth. The former things will not be remembered, nor will they come to mind.

But be glad and rejoice forever in what I will create, for
I will create Jerusalem to be a delight and its people a joy.
ISAIAH 65:17–18

Likewise, no one in the field should go back for anything.
Remember Lot's wife!
LUKE 17:31–32

Keep your eyes on Jesus, who both began and finished this race we're in . . .
he never lost sight of where he was headed—that exhilarating finish in and
with God—he could put up with anything along the way: Cross, shame,
whatever. And now he's there, in the place of honor, right alongside God.
HEBREWS 12:2 (MSG)

But in keeping with his promise we are looking forward to a new heaven
and a new earth, the home of righteousness.
2 PETER 3:13

Let the past sleep, but let it sleep on the bosom of Christ.
Leave the irreparable past in his hands, and step out
into the irresistible future with Him.[67]
OSWALD CHAMBERS

MEDITATION

Many of us learned the hard way that looking back can be detrimental to our well-being. If we look back while walking, we can easily miss a step or a raised crack in the sidewalk and find ourselves unexpectedly sprawled out and injured.

The most famous instance in the Bible of someone looking back to their detriment is the account of Lot's wife, who looked back toward her home in Sodom one last time and was instantly turned into a pillar of salt (Genesis 19:26). Yet can't we understand her longing to catch a last glimpse of the home where she had nurtured her family? So often survivors of home-destroying wildfires take one last photo before evacuating the premises—not knowing if they will ever see their homes again.

Looking back is understandable, but we must be careful not to let our backward glances linger too long. None of us would have wanted to wander in the desert for forty years as the Israelites did after leaving Egypt. No doubt we too would have tired of a daily diet of manna and been concerned about a limited supply of water. Maybe we also would have grumbled and wailed, *"If only we had meat to eat! We remember the fish we ate in Egypt at no cost—also the cucumbers, melons, leeks, onions and garlic. But now we have lost our appetite; we never see anything but this manna!"* (Numbers 11:4–6).

Oh, how selective their memories were. Did they not also remember long hours in the hot sun making bricks and digging trenches under the cruel whips of Pharaoh's taskmasters? Did they not remember Moses leading them out of that agony and God parting the Red Sea so they could escape? Nope. They just remembered the fish and the cucumbers.

We can be like those Israelites when we talk about the good old days—remembering the good but forgetting the bad. There is value in looking back over our lives to remember the spiritual milestones that marked our paths and the blessings we received. But as believers in Jesus Christ, our real joy is found in focusing on the future. We have a living hope the life we are living now will pale in comparison to the life we have waiting for us with Him in eternity. Leave the joy and the pain of the past behind and look forward.

For Reflection or Discussion

- Is there anything in your life that keeps you tethered to the past?
- How can we keep the best of the past a part of us, without getting stuck in the past?
- What do you most look forward to in the future?

A Thought to Share

> *Glimpse the past in your rearview mirror,*
> *but focus on where you are going.*

SUGGESTION FOR THE WEEK

Spend some time thinking about events in your past that shaped you into the person you are today. Then shift your focus to everything you appreciate now and all you hope for in the future.

SUGGESTED HYMNS

- O God, Our Help in Ages Past
- This Is the Day

PRAYER REQUESTS AND CLOSING PRAYER

LESSON 50

Promise Keeper

KEY VERSE

*The LORD is faithful to all his promises and
loving toward all he has made.*
PSALM 145:13

OPENING PRAYER

O LORD, HOW OFTEN WE HAVE been hurt or disappointed by broken promises. How grateful we are that we can be sure that every promise You have made to us will be fulfilled in Your time and in Your way. In Jesus' name, amen.

INTRODUCTION

A grandmother who was feeding her grandson in his high chair had to help him hold his head up to eat, as he was afflicted with cerebral palsy from birth. Wrapping her gnarled pinky finger around his tiny one, she said, "I will never give up on you. Pinky swear." It was a generational promise.

We all remember making promises when we were children, but we didn't learn to take our promises as seriously as we should until we were much older. The first serious promise many of us made was when we stood in front of a preacher in a church next to our beloved and promised to love and cherish that person "till death do us part." Yet some brides must have had their fingers crossed under their trailing bouquets and some grooms had theirs crossed behind their backs. Or else the death that gave them permission to leave was the death of the marriage, not necessarily of the people in it. Regardless, a broken marriage is a very painful broken promise.

What other promises are prevalent in our society? We have the money-back guarantee when we buy a product, a promise of sorts. We have promissory notes spelling out the details of the agreement when we take out a loan. Or a promise ring might signify an exclusive relationship between a boy and girl too young to marry.

We call out to a friend at church, "I promise I'll call you next week and we'll get together for lunch." But then we forget, or other activities fill up the week, and the promise for fellowship remains unfulfilled. We don't mean to be promise breakers. We'd rather think of ourselves as promise keepers, but none of us has a perfect record in that regard.

Who does? The only One who can claim such perfection is God. All His promises are golden, and never will He break a promise He makes to His people as a group or to each of us individually. We can count on God to keep His promises even if everyone else disappoints us.

For Reflection or Discussion

- Do you recall a time when someone broke a promise they made to you or a time you broke a promise you made to someone else?
- Were you able to offer or receive forgiveness for the broken promise? Why or why not?
- How does making a promise matter more than just saying you will do something?

Scriptures and Quotes

Then they believed his promises and sang his praise.
PSALM 106:12

My comfort in my suffering is this: Your promise preserves my life.
PSALM 119:50

*Yet he [Abraham] did not waver through unbelief regarding the promise
of God, but was strengthened in his faith and gave glory to God, being
fully persuaded that God had power to do what he had promised.*
ROMANS 4:20–21

*For no matter how many promises God has made,
they are "Yes" in Christ.*
2 CORINTHIANS 1:20

*Let us hold unswervingly to the hope we profess,
for he who promised is faithful.*
HEBREWS 10:23

*Through these he has given us his very great and precious promises, so that
through them you may participate in the divine nature and escape the
corruption in the world caused by evil desires.*
2 PETER 1:4

*The Lord is not slow in keeping his promise, as some understand slowness.
He is patient with you, not wanting anyone to perish, but everyone to
come to repentance.*
2 PETER 3:9

And this is what he promised us—even eternal life.
1 JOHN 2:25

*God embeds a promise in his word. When we keep Scripture central in
our life, spending time in it, pondering its points, honoring the way laid
out as being the righteous and holy path, then you will . . . ! There's the
promise: For then you will make your way prosperous, and then you will
have good success (Joshua 1:8).[68]*
CYNDY SHERWOOD

MEDITATION

Each time we pick up our Bibles, regardless of where the pages
fall open, we can look down and read some of the promises of God.
In a sense, His holy Word is one big promise to us from beginning
to end: I made you, I love you, and I will bring you home to Me.
Publishers have also compiled little guidebooks one can use to look

up God's promises grouped by subject matter. Afraid? Here are God's promises about fear. Lonely? Here are God's promises about loneliness, and on and on. There are thousands of promises from God in these handy little volumes, all from the pages of the Holy Bible.

Throughout history, God made some promises that were of such magnitude they were called covenants. Scholars and theologians differ on which promises should be called covenants, but we remember God promised Noah he would never destroy the world by flood again and sent a rainbow to seal His promise. He promised Abraham his people would be God's people and would prosper. He promised David his offspring would rule after him and establish God's kingdom on earth. Then there is the New Covenant promise to which we cling so tightly: Jesus came that we might have eternal life. God's best promise to us is that we will dwell with Him forever once we believe in His Son Jesus and ask Him to be our Lord and Savior.

Grasping hold of a promise from God improves every situation in which we find ourselves. The promises recorded in the Bible are for all to see, but sometimes He speaks a special promise deep into our souls that is meant just for us. He might promise, "Hold on just a little longer and you will understand what I am doing."

We can trust God's promises, but can He trust ours? How many times have we said, "God, I promise I will never do that again," only to fall victim to our own weakness? Maybe we promise to keep the Ten Commandments, especially the one about having no other god before Him, and then realize we've allowed false idols to creep into our lives.

No, we aren't always perfect promise keepers but, praise God, He is. He promises to forgive us our broken promises when we turn to Him in sincere repentance. He is our Promise Keeper.

FOR REFLECTION OR DISCUSSION

- What Bible verses do you turn to when you need to remember God's promises?
- Is there one promise from God that means the most to you as you age?
- How can you encourage others with the truth that God is a promise keeper?

A Thought to Share

A promise kept is food for the soul.

Suggestion for the Week

It's never too late to make a new promise. Relationships grow stronger when promises are fulfilled. Make a promise to a friend this week—and keep it.

Suggested Hymns

- O Jesus, I Have Promised
- Standing on the Promises of God

Prayer Requests and Closing Prayer

LESSON 51

Who Is Righteous?

KEY VERSE

> *This righteousness from God comes through faith in Jesus Christ to all who believe. There is no difference, for all have sinned and fall short of the glory of God.*
> ROMANS 3:22–23

OPENING PRAYER

O LORD, WE KNOW IN OUR hearts we are not worthy of being called righteous and never will be on our own. Thank You, Lord, that our sin became Yours, and Your righteousness became ours. We are eternally grateful. In Jesus' name, amen.

INTRODUCTION

How often did we hear our mothers say, "Who died and made you queen?" Or perhaps, "Don't break your arm patting yourself on the back." It is human nature to want to elevate ourselves above others, isn't it? To look around at people we know and say, "Well, at least I'm not like him." But such false estimations of ourselves can only lead to disappointment once reality hits. *Pride goes before destruction, a haughty spirit before a fall,* reads Proverbs 16:18 (often paraphrased simply as "pride goes before a fall") and we have all fallen.

"Righteous" is a proud, stuffy word, isn't it? It means morally upright, without guilt or sin. Even the most boastful among us might dare to think of ourselves as admirable, good at heart, or worthy in one way or another, but righteous? That's taking our opinion of ourselves a bit too far.

A church lady known for her judgmental, holier-than-thou attitude approached a male church visitor and said, "I see that red truck of yours parked outside the bar several nights a week, and I've told the pastor too! There's no mistaking that ramshackle old truck." The man didn't say anything. Just nodded and walked on. But later he parked his truck in front of the woman's house—and left it there all night.

Fortunately for believers, the Lord often checks our spirit whenever we begin to think or act like the church lady above. As soon as we find ourselves being critical of another person, we are likely to hear a still, small voice saying, "Remember, you did things like this, too, before you gave your life to Me."

Clearly any righteousness, any holiness, any purity of heart we have comes not from our own humanity but from the One who gave His life to take on our sin and give us His righteousness in return. What a wonderful transaction. What an outrageous sacrifice. What an amazing love.

For Reflection or Discussion

- Do you remember things your parents or teachers said to you to "take you down a peg or two"?
- Do you ever hear yourself sounding judgmental toward another person?
- What might help us to stop and think before judging someone else?

Scriptures and Quotes

Rejoice in the LORD and be glad, you righteous;
sing, all you who are upright in heart!
PSALM 32:11

Gray hair is a crown of splendor; it is attained by a righteous life.
PROVERBS 16:31

*The righteous flourish like the palm tree and grow like a cedar of
Lebanon. They are planted in the house of the* LORD; *they flourish in the
courts of our God. They still bear fruit in old age; they are ever full of sap
and green, to declare that the* LORD *is upright; he is my rock, and there is
no unrighteousness in him.*
PSALM 92:12–15 (ESV)

*For as the soil makes the sprout come up and a garden causes seeds to
grow, so the Sovereign* LORD *will make righteousness and praise spring up
before all nations.*
ISAIAH 61:11

*As it is written: "There is no one righteous, not even one; there is no one
who understands, no one who seeks God. All have turned away, they have
together become worthless; there is no one who does good, not even one."*
ROMANS 3:10–12

*But God demonstrates his own love for us in this: While we were still
sinners, Christ died for us.*
ROMANS 5:8

*God made him who had no sin to be sin for us, so that in him we might
become the righteousness of God.*
2 CORINTHIANS 5:21

*What is more, I consider everything a loss compared to the surpassing
greatness of knowing Christ Jesus my Lord, for whose sake I have lost all
things. I consider them rubbish, that I may gain Christ and be found in
him, not having a righteousness of my own that comes from the law, but
that which is through faith in Christ—the righteousness that comes from
God and is by faith.*
PHILIPPIANS 3:8–9

*Learn to know Christ and him crucified. Learn to sing to him and say,
"Lord Jesus, you are my righteousness, I am your sin. You took on you
what was mine; yet set on me what was yours. You became what you were
not, that I might become what I was not."* [69]
MARTIN LUTHER

MEDITATION

We all want to make a positive difference in the world—even if only in small ways within our limited circle of influence. Once we are believers in Jesus Christ, we know difference can only happen if others are drawn not just to our human attributes and characteristics but to the righteousness in us that comes from our relationship with Him. To reflect the kind of light that draws others not to us but to Him, we must first know Jesus and Him crucified. Without Him, *all our righteous acts are like filthy rags* (Isaiah 64:6).

It can be an interesting, unusual experience when Jesus' righteousness begins to creep into our behavior. We look back on a confrontation we had with someone and realize we were able to smile and walk away rather than make sure victory was ours. Hmmm . . . Jesus did that too. Or we wake up one morning and realize we have forgiven someone against whom we've held a certifiable, even well-deserved grudge for years if not decades. We forgave even without receiving an apology. Hmmm . . . Jesus taught about that kind of absolute, even if one-sided, forgiveness.

What's happening? Christ has imputed His righteousness to us. His righteousness is ours along with the Holy Spirit to guide us and the assurance of eternal life with Him in heaven, the moment we give our lives to Him. What a wonderful package of benefits.

It's never too late for us to receive these free gifts. Never too late to be righteous—to be even a little bit holy and set apart for the Lord's work. But we must believe. Now is the time to surrender your life to Jesus Christ. Now is the time to trade your sin for His righteousness. Simply pray, "Jesus, I confess I am a sinner in need of a savior. I acknowledge You are the Son of God and You died for my sins. I ask You right now to come into my heart and be my Lord and Savior. Just as I am, I surrender all to you."

Who is righteous? You are, if you prayed that prayer or one like it today or at any point in your life. Jesus traded His righteousness for your sin. Live as a righteous, grateful, redeemed child of God—one destined to spend eternity with Him.

For Reflection or Discussion

- How does it make you feel to know you can be righteous, holy, and set apart?
- What changes in thought or behavior have you experienced due to the righteousness of Jesus showing up in your life?
- Have you given your life to Christ? Have you exchanged your sin for His righteousness? If not, please do so now.

A Thought to Share

Better to be righteous in Jesus than to be right in the world's eyes.

Suggestion for the Week

How can we live more righteously this week without acting holier-than-thou? Whatever happens, we can ask ourselves what Jesus would do, how Jesus would respond, and do the same. The Holy Spirit will help us.

Suggested Hymns

- Holy, Holy, Holy
- I Surrender All
- Just As I Am

Prayer Requests and Closing Prayer

Life with Jesus

KEY VERSE

Abide in me, and I in you.
JOHN 15:4 (KJV)

OPENING PRAYER

O LORD, HOW LONELY WE FEEL sometimes. We long for at least one other person with whom we can have a deep heart connection—someone with whom to share our daily life. But we shouldn't despair. You have promised to fill that need for us, and we are amazingly grateful. In Your precious name we pray, amen.

INTRODUCTION

A common expression these days is that we want to "do life" with someone else. A young couple getting married looks forward to a future in which they, *together*, will build a home, raise a family, and do all the things that marriage brings. Friends connect regularly with updates on life's trials and joys, photos of family, and so on because by keeping one another informed, they are in fact sharing their lives with one another. Those in a small group studying the Bible together share prayer requests so they can pray for one another when they are apart. They all long to "do life" together.

People need people. Life is more fulfilling when we share it with others in our families, in our communities, in our schools and churches. We want to share life experiences with one another, bounce ideas off one another, encourage one another, laugh together, and cry together. Together is better than alone.

Yet older adults sometimes feel they've lost everyone with whom they used to share life. Parents are long departed. Siblings might have passed away. Spouses with whom they lived for fifty or more years might have gone on without them. The feeling of being left behind, compounded by grief, can send some into a downward spiral of depression and loneliness. Living in community with others and making new friends and acquaintances can help, but for some it's still not enough. The longing remains for a solid, permanent connection with another.

There is good news, however. Those who have asked Jesus Christ into their hearts are never alone. Jesus promises, *"I am with you always"* (Matthew 28:20). He is with us when we rise in the morning and when we lie down at night. He is with us at the doctor's office and on days when we aren't at our best. He is with us when we get bad news or good news. He is with us when we are praising Him and celebrating the future which we have with Him in heaven. Always, He is with us.

Wherever *we* are, Jesus is there. As the old hymn says we can even "come to the garden alone" and He will be there to walk with us and to talk with us. We only need speak His name, and He is there—waiting to "do life" with us.

For Reflection or Discussion

- As you look back over the years, with whom did you most enjoy sharing life?
- Is there anyone now who fills the need to "do life" with someone?
- How could you develop that kind of relationship with someone new?

Scriptures and Quotes

Why are you in despair, O my soul? And why have you become disturbed within me? Hope in God, for I shall again praise Him For the help of His presence.
Psalm 42:5 (NASB)

There is a friend who sticks closer than a brother.
PROVERBS 18:24

They will call him Immanuel—which means, "God with us."
MATTHEW 1:23

Father, I want those you have given me to be with me where I am, and to see my glory, the glory you have given me because you loved me before the creation of the world.
JOHN 17:24

For I am convinced that neither death nor life, neither angels nor demons, neither the present nor the future, nor any powers, neither height nor depth, nor anything else in all creation, will be able to separate us from the love of God that is in Christ Jesus our Lord.
ROMANS 8:38–39

The grace of the Lord Jesus be with you.
1 CORINTHIANS 16:23

If I am in fellowship with Jesus Christ and am indwelt by Him . . . nothing the world, the flesh, or the devil can do can touch me.[70]
OSWALD CHAMBERS

Being a branch to the true Vine means living with Christ, breathing with Christ, doing day-to-day life with Christ. It's the ongoing awareness of His presence, even when there's no feeling of His presence. Our lives become witness to His with-ness.[71]
BETH MOORE

At the moment of Jesus' death, there was no more need of only one place where God dwelled; for now, at our invitation, He would live in us. Imagine . . . the God of the universe could live anywhere in the universe, and He chooses to live in us.[72]
TY SALTZGIVER

MEDITATION

A young interim pastor at a rural church in Pennsylvania felt badly that he hadn't made time to visit an elderly parishioner whom he knew to be a faithful prayer warrior for the church. Finally, he was able to knock on her door and be invited in for a spot of tea. When he asked her how she was doing living all alone, she replied, "Oh, I'm never alone. Jesus is always here with me."

That's where we want to be in our relationship with Him, isn't it? To know, without a shadow of a doubt, that no matter who does or doesn't come to visit us, we are not alone. Jesus is always with us.

How do we get that assurance? How do we believe we can "do life" with Jesus, day in and day out? First, we must invite Him in as surely as the elderly woman invited the young pastor into her home. Only we invite Him into our hearts by confessing He is Lord and asking His forgiveness for our sins.

We must then invest time getting to know Him by reading all that's written about Him and who He says He is, in God's Word, and by spending time with Him in prayer, including time to just sit and listen to what He wants to say to us. As we get to know Him, we learn to trust Him, and that trust continues to grow with each passing day.

To share our life with Jesus, we must follow Him closely. We do that in our hearts, just as the disciples walked away from every other responsibility and loyalty to follow Him during His ministry on earth. We must put our relationship with Him ahead of all other relationships and callings. To imitate Him, we must love and obey Him.

We share life with Jesus when we share our innermost thoughts and feelings with Him. So, we acknowledge His presence and speak His name, Jesus, *for there is no other name under heaven given to men by which we must be saved* (Acts 4:12). We then act and speak as if He is there with us—because He is.

Jesus is the only One who will never leave you. Invite Him to share your life with you and to share His life through you, and you will never be alone again.

For Reflection or Discussion

- Do you know Jesus? If so, please share how you got to know Him so well.
- Do you believe you can trust Jesus with your life? Why or why not?
- How would your life change if you truly shared each day with Jesus?

A Thought to Share

When Jesus is at home in our hearts, we are never home alone.

Suggestion for the Week

When you are by yourself, talk to Jesus out loud. Think of Him as being there with you, because He is.

Suggested Hymns

- I Need Thee Every Hour
- In the Garden
- Jesus, Name Above All Names

Prayer Requests and Closing Prayer

Special Holiday Lessons

LESSON 53

Thankful Living

KEY VERSE

Enter his gates with thanksgiving and his courts with praise; give thanks to him and praise his name. For the LORD is good and his love endures forever; his faithfulness continues through all generations.
PSALM 100:4–5

OPENING PRAYER

O LORD, WHEN WE STOP TO consider all the blessings You have given us, we realize we can't begin to list them all! In this season of Thanksgiving, and all year long, may our lives be a reflection of our gratitude to You for Your mercy and goodness to us. In Your name we pray, amen.

INTRODUCTION

We live in a society that makes it easier to grumble than to be grateful. We must move someplace we never really wanted to live, so we grumble. We are disappointed the political candidate we support isn't elected, so we grumble. Daily aggravations can produce grumbling as well: scheduled visits are canceled, we must wait for a doctor's appointment, or we look forward to a meal only to be faced with a surly server. All these things and more give us opportunities to grumble.

We even feel justified in our grumbling, don't we? Grumbling is a given if we come from the misguided assumption life should be fair. Yet what if we change our assumption and our thinking? What if we begin to look, each and every day, not for reasons to grumble but for reasons to be grateful? What if we establish a habit of thankful living?

Ann Voskamp wrote a book titled *One Thousand Gifts* which began as a challenge from a friend to write down a thousand blessings in her life. Burdened down by the weight of a past of pain and a present with six children to care for, she struggled to come up with her list until she began noticing even the smallest of blessings: jam piled high on toast, the cry of the blue jay from high in the spruce, mail in the mailbox, wool sweaters with turtleneck collars. Do you see the switch: the change from grumbling to gratitude? Ann's list far exceeded a thousand blessings once she opened her eyes to all that was around her, and the same can be true of us.

Can we do it? Can we begin to look for opportunities to be grateful rather than opportunities to grumble? Keeping our eyes on God is a good place to start. Ann Voskamp wrote in her blog, "We will give thanks to God not because of how we feel, but because of who He is."[73] Let us give thanks.

For Reflection or Discussion

- Who do you know who is especially good at turning grumbling into gratitude?
- What keeps you from being more like this person?
- Name something you are grateful for today.

Scriptures and Quotes

Give thanks to the LORD, for he is good; his love endures forever.
PSALM 107:1

But thanks be to God! He gives us the victory through our Lord Jesus Christ.
1 CORINTHIANS 15:57

Do not be anxious about anything, but in everything, by prayer and petition, with thanksgiving, present your requests to God.
PHILIPPIANS 4:6

Give thanks in all circumstances, for this is God's will for you in Christ Jesus.
1 THESSALONIANS 5:18

Therefore, since we are receiving a kingdom that cannot be shaken, let us be thankful, and so worship God acceptably with reverence and awe.
HEBREWS 12:28

Gratitude is our ability to see the grace of God, morning by morning, no matter what else greets us in the course of the day.[74]
CRAIG BARNES

Gratitude to God makes even a temporal blessing a taste of heaven.[75]
WILLIAM ROMAINE

MEDITATION

Can we do it? Can we even convert a life of habitual grumbling into a life of thankful living? With God's help, and by keeping our focus on Him, we can. Not all of us are grumblers, but all of us can be more aware of our blessings.

The older we grow, the more blessings we have in our blessings accounts. We enter into a life of thankful living when we spend more time remembering our blessings than fretting about what we don't have now. For example, those of us blessed to be parents and grandparents can easily find ourselves wishing we could spend more time with those we love, but just the very existence of those people in our families is a blessing, isn't it?

A woman having breakfast with her husband at a restaurant entered into a discussion with their waitress and learned the waitress was excited about leaving to visit her grandchildren the next day. "How old are they?" the woman asked. "They are six and eight," the waitress replied. "How long has it been since you've seen them?" the woman inquired. "Oh, I've never seen them," the waitress answered.

That puts having to go weeks or months without seeing those we love into perspective, doesn't it?

Paul wrote his letter to the Christians in Philippi, the Book of Philippians in the Bible, while he was in prison in Rome. Paul had much to grumble about. He was falsely accused and unfairly imprisoned. Yet the Book of Philippians is known as the book of joy. Despite his circumstances, Paul was able to write a message of joy because of the certainty of his faith in Jesus Christ. His joy and gratitude were based on the eternity he knew was waiting for him, not on the prison cell around him.

We can have the same attitude of gratitude that sustained Paul. We can experience the joy of thankful living by focusing on all God has done for us—and on our eternal life to come. As Thanksgiving comes this year, let us say along with Paul, *"I thank my God"* (Philippians 1:3).

For Reflection or Discussion

- What keeps us from being able to express gratitude to others?
- Is there someone in your life to whom you can give the gift of thanks today?
- As you look back over your life, can you recall times you may have neglected to thank God for His work in your life? Thank Him now.

A Thought to Share

Thankful living begins with thanks giving.

Suggestion for the Week

This is a wonderful week to begin the habit of thankful living. Look around you and make a list of every blessing you see. Maybe you'll get to a thousand!

Suggested Hymns

Give Thanks (Contemporary Praise Song)
Now Thank We All Our God
We Gather Together

Prayer Requests and Closing Prayer

LESSON 54

The Christmas Message

KEY VERSE

"I am the Lord's servant," Mary answered. "May it be to me as you have said." Then the angel left her.
LUKE 1:38

OPENING PRAYER

O LORD, AS WE COME INTO this Christmas season, may we be as open as Mary was to accept any assignment You have for us and as faithful and fearless in accomplishing our mission. In Jesus' name, amen.

INTRODUCTION

The news came as a shock. Like any unwed teenage girl, the last thing Mary wanted to hear was that she was pregnant. The possibility had never even entered her mind. She wasn't in the bathroom with a home pregnancy test when she found out. More likely, she was kneading bread in a crude wooden bowl in the kitchen of her parents' cottage in Nazareth.

Perhaps Mary was daydreaming of her fiancé, Joseph, and their upcoming wedding when every crevice of the bare kitchen became illuminated with a heavenly light. Mary could even have had traces of flour on her face when she looked up to behold Gabriel, the angel of the Lord, in all his radiance.

God must be keenly aware of the dramatic effect His angels can have, for He instructed Gabriel to greet Mary warmly and to quickly add, *"Do not be afraid, Mary, you have found favor with God"* (Luke 1:30). Mary might have just caught her breath in time to hear: *"You will be with child and give birth to a son, and you are to give him the name Jesus. He will be great and will be called the Son of the Most High"* (Luke 1:31–32).

This Christmas let us pause to consider Mary and how she received this life-giving role, this astonishing message, she was given. She was a virgin. Her life, so full of promise just a few short minutes ago, now seemed turned upside down. Mary must have worried about what Joseph and her parents would say, but her faith sustained her. She questioned how this could be. She never faltered when the angel said the Holy Spirit would accomplish the miracle.

We would all be wise to ponder how we would have responded in Mary's sandals. Would we have been so quick to believe the angel was from God or that we had been chosen for such a divine assignment? What message might God be sending us this Christmas, and how will we respond to it?

For Reflection or Discussion

- Have you ever seen an angel? Do you know anyone who has?
- Do you believe there are angels among us?
- What do you think Mary did that day once the angel left?

Scriptures and Quotes

For to us a child is born, to us a son is given, and the government will be on his shoulders, And he will be called Wonderful Counselor, Mighty God, Everlasting Father, Prince of Peace.
Isaiah 9:6

But after he had considered this, an angel of the Lord appeared to him in a dream and said, "Joseph son of David, do not be afraid to take Mary home as your wife, because what is conceived in her is from the Holy

Spirit. She will give birth to a son, and you are to give him the name Jesus, because he will save his people from their sins."
MATTHEW 1:20–21

Do not be afraid, Mary, you have found favor with God. You will be with child and give birth to a son, and you are to give him the name Jesus.
LUKE 1:30–31

The angel answered, "The Holy Spirit will come upon you, and the power of the Most High will overshadow you. So the holy one to be born will be called the Son of God."
LUKE 1:35

"I am the Lord's servant," Mary answered. "May it be to me as you have said." Then the angel left her.
LUKE 1:38

My soul glorifies the Lord and my spirit rejoices in God my Savior, for he has been mindful of the humble state of his servant.
LUKE 1:46–48

An angel of the Lord appeared to them, and the glory of the Lord shone around them, and they were terrified. But the angel said to them, "Do not be afraid. I bring you good news of great joy that will be for all the people. Today in the town of David a Savior has been born to you; he is Christ the Lord."
LUKE 2:9–11

God always looks at the heart, not the outward appearance (1 Samuel 16:7). When he looked at dear Mary, He found in her a woman after his own heart, a woman who would live according to his will.[76]
ELIZABETH GEORGE

MEDITATION

There are those who believe Mary is truly divine and those who believe she was simply a woman chosen and blessed by God. Wherever our beliefs take us, we should all be fascinated by Mary's life and all it has to teach us about being willing to follow God's will for us.

Being pregnant for the first time is an awesome yet daunting experience in itself. How must Mary have felt knowing the baby she was carrying would not only be her son but also her Savior?

Much of the world would have us leave Mary kneeling sweetly next to Jesus, whom they would have us leave as a babe in a manger. Yet that wasn't the end of Mary's experience. Mary was still the mother of Jesus long after the lonely birth in a stable far from home.

Imagine Jesus as a little boy with younger siblings. Did Mary worry that He would fall off a donkey or run in front of a cart in the streets of Nazareth? We know she fretted when He stayed too long in the temple in Jerusalem as a twelve-year-old, but then she *treasured all these things in her heart* (Luke 2:51). Our hearts ache for her when we realize that, although she may have had Jesus at home longer than most of us have our children, she knew when He left to begin His ministry, He would never be home for the holidays.

The glimpses the Gospels give us of the rest of Mary's life include the fact she stood in heartbreaking sorrow in the shadow of the cross at Jesus' crucifixion. We read, *When Jesus saw his mother there, and the disciple whom he loved standing nearby, he said to his mother, "Dear woman, here is your son," and to the disciple, "Here is your mother"* (John 19:26–27). Jesus cared for her from the cross. She who heard Jesus take His first breath on earth also heard Him breathe His last when He died to save us all.

God's final gift of grace to this faithful, grieving mother may have been when He made sure the disciples got word to her after the resurrection that they had seen Jesus, and He was indeed alive! Later, she became a part of the first group of believers who met and prayed regularly together (Acts 1:14).

Mary was open to the plans God had for her. This year may we all have a Merry Christmas—and A Mary Christmas, one filled with peace, hope, and the knowledge that God can accomplish much in the world through us.

For Reflection or Discussion

- How do you imagine Jesus as a little boy or adolescent?
- Do you think Mary worried about Him?
- What part of Mary's character would you like to emulate?

A Thought to Share

Listen for unexpected messages this Christmas.

Suggestion for the Week

This week talk to young mothers you know about Mary, the mother of Jesus, and remind them they, too, are blessed.

Suggested Hymns

- Away in a Manger
- Hark! The Herald Angels Sing
- Silent Night

Prayer Requests and Closing Prayer

LESSON 55

That's Love

KEY VERSE

Dear friends, let us love one another, for love comes from God. Everyone who loves has been born of God and knows God. Whoever does not love does not know God, because God is love.
1 JOHN 4:7–8

OPENING PRAYER

O LORD, WE KNOW THAT TO love others unconditionally and fully, we must first love You and know You as our personal Savior. Help us to love as You love and to be conduits of Your love to all those we encounter. In Jesus' name, amen.

INTRODUCTION

Valentines, chocolates, red roses in a lovely vase—all these things say "I love you" on Valentine's Day. There's more to love, though, isn't there? It isn't just romantic love that deserves celebration on this special day, but all the ways love is expressed in our world. Let us count the ways.

A two-year-old stops playing with her tea set and races to the door when the doorbell rings because she knows it might be her mom coming to get her. That's love.

A badly injured dog struggles to walk across the room at the veterinary clinic where she is fighting for her life to lay her head on the shoulder of her worried owner sitting on the floor waiting for her. That's love.

Two women who normally attend an assisted living Bible study are conspicuously absent. The leader learns one of the women isn't feeling well and the other wants to sit with her. That's love.

A mom gazes amazed into the eyes of her newborn son during the "getting to know you" stage of their lifelong relationship. That's love.

A homeless man divides a roll he was given with hands wearing holey mittens and gives half to his homeless friend next to him. That's love.

A woman with a houseful of kids to feed takes the time to make some soup for the elderly neighbor next door who is ailing. That's love.

A husband visits his wife in a care facility every day even though she no longer remembers him or their sixty-year marriage. That's love.

A woman who recently lost her husband comes home to find her family has beautifully decorated her home and yard for the Christmas season. That's love.

A weary mom volunteers for extra carpool duty because she knows her friend is going through a hard time. That's love.

In 1 John 4:19 we read, *We love because he first loved us.* That's the kind of love we can see in our world when we look for it—the kind of love worth celebrating on Valentine's Day and every day.

For Reflection or Discussion

- Do you do anything special to celebrate Valentine's Day? If so, what?
- Can you recall a special Valentine's Day from years past?
- How would you define real love?

Scriptures and Quotes

Love the LORD your God with all your heart
and with all your soul and with all your strength.
DEUTERONOMY 6:5

"Teacher, which is the greatest commandment in the Law?" Jesus replied:
" 'Love the Lord your God with all your heart and with all your soul and

with all your mind.' This is the first and greatest commandment. And the second is like it: 'Love your neighbor as yourself.'"
MATTHEW 22:36–39

For God so loved the world that he gave his one and only Son, that whoever believes in him shall not perish but have eternal life.
JOHN 3:16

By this all men will know that you are my disciples, if you love one another.
JOHN 13:35

My command is this: Love each other as I have loved you.
JOHN 15:12

But God demonstrates his own love for us in this: While we were still sinners, Christ died for us.
ROMANS 5:8

How great is the love the Father has lavished on us, that we should be called children of God! And that is what we are!
1 JOHN 3:1

This is how we know what love is: Jesus Christ laid down his life for us.
1 JOHN 3:16

We love because he first loved us.
1 JOHN 4:19

God has created us to do small things with great love. I believe in that great love, that comes, or should come from our heart, should start at home: with my family, my neighbors across the street, those right next door. And this love should then reach everyone.[77]
MOTHER TERESA

MEDITATION

Of all the places in the Bible that talk about love, the thirteenth chapter of First Corinthians is known as the "love passage." In it, Paul describes love as patient, kind, not envious or boastful, not proud, rude, self-seeking or easily angered. He says love keeps no record of wrongs, does not delight in evil but rejoices with the truth. Moreover, love always protects, always trusts, always hopes, always perseveres, and never fails (1 Corinthians 13:4–8). Paul was writing to believers in Corinth, but the Word is speaking to us about loving in this way today.

Young couples getting married often choose this passage to be read at their weddings—even those who may not have studied the Bible at all—just because they know the content is appropriate for the occasion. We should pray they will go back and read the passage again, paying close attention to Paul's instruction, so his description of love can become the basis for a long-lasting marriage.

Yet who of us can live up to Paul's standard of loving, as described in this passage? Truly no one can unless he or she first draws from the unending source of God's love, unless the Holy Spirit supplies all the love needed for any and every situation.

Once we understand the nature of God's love, we will understand how calling on His love to fill us up will make it so much easier to love others. God's love is unconditional, meaning there is nothing we can do to make Him love us less and nothing we can do to make Him love us more. God demonstrated His love for us by sending Christ to die for our sins so we may dwell with Him forever.

God's love is trustworthy. It will never fail us. God will never say, "I can't help you love that difficult person, you're on your own." Rather He will say, once we ask Him for help, "Sure, take some of My love, and give it generously."

1 Corinthians 13 ends with verse 13: *And now these three remain: faith, hope and love. But the greatest of these is love.* What a sad world this would be without love. Let's celebrate it on Valentine's Day and every day, and praise God for giving it to us in abundance.

For Reflection or Discussion

- Looking at Paul's description of love in 1 Corinthians 13:4–8, are there some aspects of love that you find more difficult to reflect to others? Why?
- Do you believe deep down in your soul that God loves you? If not, ask Him to reassure you of His love.
- Who do you know who may need a strong dose of God's love, delivered through you?

A Thought to Share

Never forget that you are God's valentine—now and forever.

Suggestion for the Week

Spend some time this week looking up verses about love in your Bible. Thank the Lord for loving you the way He does and feel His warm embrace around you.

Suggested Hymns

- Jesus Loves Me
- O, How I Love Jesus
- They'll Know We Are Christians by Our Love

Prayer Requests and Closing Prayer

LESSON 56

The Cross at Easter

KEY VERSE

Carrying his own cross, he went out to the place of the Skull (which in Aramaic is called Golgotha). Here they crucified him, and with him two others—one on each side and Jesus in the middle.
JOHN 19:17–18

OPENING PRAYER

LORD JESUS, WE CAN NEVER fully appreciate the sacrifice You made for us on the cross, but we will be eternally grateful to You. Help us turn our hearts and minds in the direction of the cross this Easter season, as we celebrate the glorious truth that, though You died for us, death could not hold You! In Your mighty name we pray, amen.

INTRODUCTION

The cross is an iconic symbol in our world. When we look for it, we see its familiar shape everywhere: in the pattern on a six-panel door, in the crisscrossed hatches of a windowpane, even in the shape of a bird soaring in flight above us. The cross symbol is ubiquitous.

Since ancient times various shapes of crosses have existed. The Greek cross has four equal arms; the Latin cross has a base stem longer than the other three arms; St. Anthony's cross is shaped like the letter T, and an X-shaped cross is known as St. Andrew's cross. The Jerusalem cross has four arms of equal length, with a Greek cross in each quadrant formed. It is said to represent Christ's command to spread the gospel around the world—to the north, the south, the east, and the west—a mission that started in Jerusalem.

Many believers wear a cross necklace to signify Christ's sacrifice on the cross, while others think it was such a device of torture in Roman times that we might just as soon wear a guillotine around our necks. Even nonbelievers wear crosses as fashion statements, without attaching any meaning to them at all. If only they knew. The value is not in the cross itself, but in what it represents.

Most scholars think Jesus was probably crucified on a Latin cross, with the longer vertical beam, and so that's the cross so often shown in artists' depictions of the crucifixion scene. What matters most, however, is not the type of cross Jesus died on, but that He died for you and for me.

Easter is a wonderful time to spiritually come to the cross and relinquish all the fears and anxieties that plague us. Easter is also a time to reflect on the greatest sacrifice of all time and to personally acknowledge, with great gratitude, what that sacrifice means to each one of us. It's a time to fully accept the redemption and forgiveness offered to us through Jesus Christ.

For Reflection or Discussion

- Look around you now. Where do you see the cross symbol?
- Is it important to you to know on what kind of cross Christ died?
- Is wearing a cross necklace, or other cross jewelry, meaningful to you? Why or why not?

Scriptures and Quotes

For he bore the sin of many, and made intercession for the transgressors.
Isaiah 53:12

If anyone would come after me, he must deny himself and take up his cross and follow me. For whoever wants to save his life will lose it, but whoever loses his life for me and for the gospel will save it.
Mark 8:34–35

Jesus said, "Father, forgive them, for they do not know what they are doing." And they divided up his clothes by casting lots.
LUKE 23:34

But God raised him from the dead, freeing him from the agony of death, because it was impossible for death to keep its hold on him.
ACTS 2:24

For the message of the cross is foolishness to those who are perishing, but to us who are being saved it is the power of God.
1 CORINTHIANS 1:18

He himself bore our sins in his body on the tree, so that we might die to sins and live for righteousness; by his wounds you have been healed.
1 PETER 2:24

The cross is the only ladder high enough to touch Heaven's threshold.[78]
GEORGE DANA BOARDMAN

Carry the cross patiently, and with perfect submission; and in the end it shall carry you.[79]
THOMAS À KEMPIS

Nothing in my hand I bring, Simply to Thy cross I cling.[80]
AUGUSTUS M. TOPLADY

MEDITATION

In a sense, the entire Christian life is a series of steps closer and closer to the Cross of Calvary—with each step an arrival. Only as we draw close in prayer and meditation to the truth of what Christ did for us by willingly dying on that cross can we realize the enormity of the gift God gave us. For many, that journey is a lifelong process.

We can see the love Christ displayed on the cross even from a distance, where we may have stood terrified and huddled together under some tree on that dark day of crucifixion. We see the love for His mother as He asked the Apostle John to care for her once He was gone. We see the love for the believing thief on the cross next to Him as He promised, *"Today you will be with me in paradise"*

(Luke 23:43). We see His love for every man and woman created by His Father throughout history and beyond as He made the ultimate sacrifice for mankind. His sacrifice expressed His love for you and for me.

What do we see as we draw closer? Jesus didn't *just* pay the price for our sin, rather He *took on* all the sin of the world so nobody anywhere would have to suffer eternal consequences for being less than perfect. When John the Baptist first saw Jesus on the shore of the Jordan River he said, *"Look, the Lamb of God, who takes away the sin of the world!"* (John 1:29). Believe. Come to the cross, and your sin, past, present, and future, is gone—not rationalized or sugarcoated in some way. Gone. As is the guilt of that sin. You are completely forgiven.

One step closer and we see the abject humility of the one who is both the Son of God and the Son of Man. We see His wounds and the blood flowing down. He lowered Himself to the very pit of hell—separation from God—so we might go higher than we could ever go on our own. *And being found in appearance as a man, he humbled himself and became obedient to death—even death on a cross!* (Philippians 2:8).

The Bible promises if we also humble ourselves in the eyes of the Lord, He will lift us up. Are you there at the foot of the cross? There's no better time than this Easter to take that journey. Fall to your knees in humility and worship the One whose resurrection from the dead we celebrate on Easter Sunday. Accept His unconditional forgiveness and love. You are welcome at the foot of the cross.

For Reflection or Discussion

- Love, sacrifice, forgiveness, and humility are all displayed by Jesus on the cross. Which means the most to you this Easter and why?
- Did anything in today's lesson draw you closer to the cross? If so, explain.
- Do you feel you've made the journey to the foot of the cross? If not, what will you do to step closer?

A Thought to Share

The ground is level at the foot of the cross,
and there's always room for one more.

Suggestion for the Week

Look for the shape of the cross in your environment this week. Each time you see a cross, thank Jesus for sacrificing His life for you.

Suggested Hymns

- Nothing but the Blood of Jesus
- The Old Rugged Cross
- When I Survey the Wondrous Cross

Prayer Requests and Closing Prayer

LESSON 57

We Pledge Allegiance

KEY VERSE

Blessed is the nation whose God is the LORD,
the people he chose for his inheritance.
PSALM 33:12

OPENING PRAYER

O LORD, HOW GRATEFUL WE ARE for this country in which we live. We implore You to forgive us for all the many ways we have failed to acknowledge Your hand in our very existence. We cherish our country, Lord, but it is to You we give all allegiance and honor forever. In Jesus' name, amen.

INTRODUCTION

Most of us can remember beginning each school day standing by our desks with our hands over our hearts and reciting The Pledge of Allegiance to the flag of the United States of America. We stood a bit taller the first day of school in our plaid dresses and stiff jeans as we recited those well-revered words. Maybe later in the year, on a truly special day, we got to go to the front of the classroom to stand by the flag and lead the class in the saying of the pledge.

Patriots among us still watch for opportunities to stand and say the pledge, even as we sadly see those opportunities dwindle. First, there was an effort to remove the words "under God" from the pledge, then fewer and fewer schools kept the reciting of the pledge as a part of each school day. Yet those words forever in our hearts still sound out every US citizen's allegiance to our country.

There's an adage which says if you don't stand for something, you'll fall for anything. What we need to remember, however, even in our later years, is that it makes a big difference for what we choose to stand. We need to choose our loyalties carefully, and then put our hearts and souls into defending those choices till the end of our days.

On national holidays like Independence Day (July 4), Veterans Day, and Memorial Day, the stars and stripes of the grand ol' flag of the United States are more prominent and fly most proudly. It's important for us to pause on these patriotic holidays to thank God for creating and protecting this wonderful country that we have the privilege of calling home. Each celebration offers another opportunity to stand up for our country, whether by displaying a flag of our own or putting our hands over our hearts as the flag marches by on parade.

Yes, it's important for us to pledge allegiance to our country and never take her freedoms and benefits for granted. But even more important is our allegiance to the God under whom our country was created. Our true allegiance, our undying loyalty once we are believers in Him and His Son Jesus Christ, must be always and only to the King of Kings, the Lord of Lords. After all, our true citizenship is in heaven.

For Reflection or Discussion

- What memories do you have of saying The Pledge of Allegiance in school as a child?
- Do you remember when the words "under God" were added in 1954 at the urging of President Dwight D. Eisenhower?
- Are there other countries or organizations to which you have pledged your allegiance?

Scriptures and Quotes

What other nation is so great as to have their gods near them the way the Lord our God is near us whenever we pray to him?
Deuteronomy 4:7

May the nations be glad and sing for joy, for you rule the peoples justly and guide the nations of the earth.
PSALM 67:4

Many nations will come and say, "Come, let us go up to the mountain of the LORD, to the house of the God of Jacob. He will teach us his ways, so that we may walk in his paths."
MICAH 4:2

It is for freedom that Christ has set us free. Stand firm, then, and do not let yourselves be burdened again by a yoke of slavery.
GALATIANS 5:1

Consequently, you are no longer foreigners and aliens, but fellow citizens with God's people and members of God's household, built on the foundation of the apostles and prophets, with Christ Jesus himself as the chief cornerstone.
EPHESIANS 2:19–20

But our citizenship is in heaven. And we eagerly await a Savior from there, the Lord Jesus Christ.
PHILIPPIANS 3:20

But you are a chosen people, a royal priesthood, a holy nation, a people belonging to God, that you may declare the praises of him who called you out of darkness into his wonderful light.
1 PETER 2:9

I pledge allegiance to the flag of the United States of America, and to the republic for which it stands, one nation under God, indivisible, with liberty and justice for all.
THE PLEDGE OF ALLEGIANCE

It is the duty of all Nations to acknowledge the providence of Almighty God, to obey his will, to be grateful for his benefits, and humbly to implore his protection and favor.[81]
GEORGE WASHINGTON

MEDITATION

The verses we read in the Bible describing a great nation are usually referring to the nation of Israel, God's chosen people, but because we as believers are also chosen, we, too, are members of the citizenship of heaven. The United States of America is not mentioned in God's holy Word at all, but our Judeo-Christian roots tie us forever to the nation of Israel, and that is why so many Christians defend Israel against her attackers even today.

Just as we study American history to learn all the reasons which we have to pledge allegiance to our country, so we study biblical history to understand our great inheritance from the Lord.

We celebrate American war heroes, and we honor those heroes and heroines of the faith listed in Hebrews 11. We admire our astronauts and first responders, and we draw strength from the humility and repentance of King David (Psalm 32) or the courage of Queen Esther (Esther 4). Our allegiance to our country and her history can co-exist quite harmoniously with our allegiance to the history of our faith and of our Lord God.

Yet we must never forget which allegiance is greater—which allegiance carries with it an eternal citizenship and the guarantee we will *dwell in the house of the Lord forever* (Psalm 23:6). That's our loyalty and allegiance to God the Father, the Son, and the Holy Spirit.

What does it mean to be a citizen of heaven? What would the passport of such a citizen look like? Maybe it would glow with a heavenly light. It would grant us full entrance to the streets of gold and include a map showing us just where our heavenly mansion is located. That's our limited, human imagination at work. But the truth is, we can never fully know the extent of the blessings and benefits of being citizens of heaven until we arrive. We only know that all our allegiance and loyalty forever rightly belong to the God who has promised to take us there.

FOR REFLECTION OR DISCUSSION

- What heroes from American history or from the Bible do you recall most often?

- In a sense, all believers have dual citizenship. Do you believe it's right and good to offer your allegiance to a country as well as to God?
- What do you imagine your citizenship in heaven will include?

A Thought to Share

We stand for the flag and kneel at the cross.

Suggestion for the Week

Ask people with whom you engage in conversation if they remember The Pledge of Allegiance, and give them an opportunity to recite it for you. Remind them they are citizens of a wonderful country and can also be citizens of heaven.

Suggested Hymns

- God Bless America
- My Country, 'Tis of Thee
- Stand Up, Stand Up for Jesus

Prayer Requests and Closing Prayer

Notes

1   Robert Durback, ed., *Seeds of Hope: A Henri Nouwen Reader* (New York: Doubleday, 1997), 188.

2   Margaret Willour, *Reader's Digest* (1982), found at www. http://thinkexist.com/quotes/margaret_willour/.

3   Nancy Leigh DeMoss, *Holiness: The Heart God Purifies* (Chicago: Moody, 2005), 142.

4   Frank S. Mead, *12,000 Religious Quotations* (Grand Rapids: Baker Book House, 1989), 228.

5   David Roper, "The Good Old Days," *Our Daily Bread* (Grand Rapids: RBC Ministries, 2013), January 28.

6   Oswald Chambers, *My Utmost for His Highest* (Westwood, NJ: Barbour, 1963), 306.

7   Beth Lueders, *Two Days Longer* (West Monroe, LA: Howard, 2006), 6.

8   L. B. Cowman, *Streams in the Desert* (Grand Rapids: Zondervan, 1997), 113.

9   Chambers, *My Utmost for His Highest*, 205.

10 C. S. Lewis, *The Lion, the Witch and the Wardrobe* (New York: HarperTrophy, 1950, 1978), 86.

11 Harry Verploegh, ed., *Oswald Chambers: The Best from All His Books* (Nashville: Thomas Nelson, 1987), 8.

12 Mother Teresa, "Saints Among Us: The Work of Mother Teresa," *Time* magazine, December 29, 1975, http://content.time.com/time/subscriber/article/0,33009,945463-5,00.html.

13 Verploegh, *Oswald Chambers*, 213.

14 Priscilla Shirer, *Discerning the Voice of God* (Nashville: Lifeway, 2018), 149.

15 Henry Drummond, *"Beautiful Thoughts" from Henry Drummond*, arr. Elizabeth Cureton (New York: James Pott, 1893), 242.

16 Gershom Gorenberg, *The End of Days: Fundamentalism and the Struggle for the Temple Mount* (New York: Oxford University Press, 2000), 11.

17 Madeleine L'Engle, *Glimpses of Grace: Daily Thoughts and Reflections* (New York: HarperSanFrancisco, 1996), 104.

18 Verploegh, *Oswald Chambers*, 234.

19 Cowman, *Streams in the Desert*, 28.

20 John Henry Jowett, *The Silver Lining: Messages of Hope and Cheer* (Minneapolis: Curiosmith, 2016), 80.

21 Billy Graham, "Answers," Billy Graham Evangelistic Association, May 16, 2008, https://billygraham.org/answer/do-you-believe-in-death-bed-conversions.

22 Verploegh, *Oswald Chambers*, 30.

23 Chambers, *My Utmost for His Highest*, 65.

24 John Ortberg, *Soul Keeping: Caring for the Most Important Part of You* (Grand Rapids: Zondervan, 2014), 190.

25 Dallas Willard, *Hearing God* (Downers Grove, IL: IVP Books, 2012), 20–21.

26 Verploegh, *Oswald Chambers*, 202.

27 François Fénelon, *Selections from the Writings of Fenelon with a Memoir of His Life* (Boston: Hilliard, Gray, Little, and Wilkins, 1831), 226–27.

28 Helen Keller, *The Open Door* (New York: Doubleday, 1957), 15.

29 Ron R. Ritchie, "Just Because You're Breathing Doesn't Mean You're Living," Ron R. Ritchie (blog), March 1, 2008, http://ronritchie.blogspot.com/.

30 Robert A. Jonas, ed., *The Essential Henri Nouwen* (Boston: Shambhala, 2009), 147.

31 Charles Noel Douglas, comp., *Forty Thousand Quotations: Prose and Poetical* (New York: Halcyon, 1917); Bartleby.com, 2012, www.bartleby.com/348/.

32   Tryon Edwards, ed., *A Dictionary of Thoughts: Being a Cyclopedia of Laconic Quotations* (Detroit: F. B. Dickerson, 1908), 215.

33   Tim McConnell, *Happy Church* (Downers Grove, IL: InterVarsity, 2016), 22–23.

34   George Whitefield, "The Folly and Danger of Being Not Righteous Enough," Christian Classics Ethereal Library, https://www.ccel.org/ccel/whitefield/sermons.xi.html.

35   Mead, *12,000 Religious Quotations*, 450.

36   Abram N. Coleman, ed., *Proverbial Wisdom: Proverbs, Maxims, and Ethical Sentences*, 3rd ed., (New York: Peter Eckler, 1903), 10.

37   Cyndy Sherwood, *Healing Words* (Colorado Springs: Promise Land, 2015), 353.

38   Edwards, *Dictionary of Thoughts*, 87.

39   Robert Herrick, *The Poems of Robert Herrick* (London: Grant Richards, 1902), 326.

40   Shirer, *Discerning the Voice of God*, 181–82.

41   Mother Teresa, *In My Own Words*, comp. José Luis González-Balado (New York: Random House, 1997), 94.

42   Cynthia Heald, *Becoming a Woman Whose God Is Enough* (Colorado Springs: NavPress, 2014), 31.

43   Charles R. Swindoll, *Swindoll's Living Insights: New Testament Commentary JOHN* (Carol Stream, IL: Tyndale, 2010), 92.

44   Heald, *Becoming a Woman Whose God Is Enough*, 28.

45   W. Phillip Keller, *A Shepherd Looks at Psalm 23* (Grand Rapids: Zondervan, 2007), 17–18.

46   Missy Buchanan, *Voices of Aging* (Nashville: Upper Room, 2015), 41.

47   Buchanan, *Voices of Aging*, 49.

48   Buchanan, *Voices of Aging*, 25.

49   John Newton, quoted in *The Christian Spectator*, vol. 3 (New Haven: S. Converse, 1821), 186.

278 | *The Hope of Glory*

50   Priscilla Shirer, *The Armor of God* (Nashville: Lifeway, 2019), 178.

51   William Jerdan, *The Works of the Rev. George Herbert* (London: George Routledge, 1853), 386.

52   Cecil Frances Alexander, "All Things Bright and Beautiful," *Baptist Hymnal* (1991), 46.

53   Kirkie Morrissey, "The Importance, Power, and Value of Praise," (lecture, Fellowship of the Rockies Church, Colorado Springs, n.d.).

54   Ruth Myers, *31 Days of Praise* (Sisters, OR: Multnomah, 1994), 119.

55   Heald, *Becoming a Woman Whose God Is Enough*, 167.

56   George MacDonald, *Annals of a Quiet Neighborhood* (Bibliotech, 2019), 198.

57   Sherwood, *Healing Words*, 365.

58   Charles Spurgeon, "A Wafer of Honey" (sermon, Metropolitan Tabernacle, London, 1863).

59   Chambers, *My Utmost for His Highest*, 20.

60   Alexander Pope, "Universal Prayer," *Hymns for Public Worship* (1845), 414.

61   *Great Is Thy Faithfulness: 365 Devotions from Our Daily Bread* (Grand Rapids: Discovery House, 2009), October 31.

62   Nancy Parker Brummett and Alice Scott-Ferguson, *Reconcilable Differences: Two Friends Debate God's Roles for Women* (Colorado Springs: David C. Cook, 2006).

63   Cyndy Sherwood, *Running Words* (Colorado Springs: Promise Land, 2019), 248.

64   Henri J. M. Nouwen and Walter J. Gaffney, *Aging: The Fulfillment of Life* (New York: Doubleday, 1974), 13.

65   Richard J. Foster, *Prayer: Finding the Heart's True Home* (San Francisco: HarperCollins, 1992), 15.

66   Beth Moore, *Chasing Vines* (Carol Stream, IL: Tyndale, 2020), 136.

67   Chambers, *My Utmost for His Highest*, 366.

68   Sherwood, *Running Words*, 97.

69   Martin Luther, *Letters of a Spiritual Counsel*, in *Library of Christian Classics*, vol. 18, ed. Theodore G. Tappert (London: SCM, 1955), 110.

70   Verploegh, *Oswald Chambers*, 117.

71   Moore, *Chasing Vines*, 142.

72   Ty Saltzgiver, *40 Days of Lent* (Colorado Springs: Salt Resources, 2017), Day 37.

73   Ann Voskamp, "The Holy Experience," Nov. 25, 2013. https://annvoskamp.com/blog/.

74   Craig Barnes, *Hustling God* (Grand Rapids: Zondervan, 2001), 182.

75   Edwards, *Dictionary of Thoughts*, 206.

76   Elizabeth George, *The Remarkable Women of the Bible* (Eugene, OR: Harvest House, 2003), 208.

77   Mother Teresa, *In My Own Words*, 45.

78   George Dana Broadman, *Epiphanies of the Risen Lord* (New York: D. Appleton, 1879), 64–65.

79   Edwards, *Dictionary of Thoughts*, 98.

80   Augustus M. Toplady, "Rock of Ages," *Baptist Hymnal* (Convention Press, 1991), 342.

81   George Washington, "Thanksgiving Proclamation of 1789," Mount Vernon (website), https://www.mountvernon.org/education/primary-sources-2/article/thanksgiving-proclamation-of-1789/.

About the Author

Nancy Parker Brummett first led a Bible study in an assisted living setting in 1999, and she and the Lord developed *The Hope of Glory*, Volumes One and Two, in the years following. She gained a heart for older adults as a child because her grandmother lived with her family, and she has enjoyed close friendships with many older adults over the years. She also journeyed with her mother and mother-in-law through their assisted living experiences, and her academic interest in aging led her to receive the Professional Advancement Certificate in Gerontology from the University of Colorado at Colorado Springs.

An author and freelance writer living in Colorado Springs, Nancy's other books include *Simply the Savior, It Takes a Home, The Journey of Elisa, Reconcilable Differences, Take My Hand Again: A Faith-Based Guide for Helping Aging Parents*, and *The Hope of Glory*, Volume One. She focuses her writing and speaking ministries on her passion for older adults and those who care for them. Nancy lives in Colorado Springs, CO, with her husband Jim. They have four grown children, twelve grandchildren, and two great-grandchildren in their blended family. To learn more about Nancy's life and work or to subscribe to her blogs, visit her website at www.nancyparkerbrummett.com.

www.ingramcontent.com/pod-product-compliance
Lightning Source LLC
Chambersburg PA
CBHW070023100426
42740CB00013B/2579